THE MAGIC & MYSTERY OF
SCOTLAND

Biographies and Acknowledgements

To my wife Dorothy, for her support over the years
Dennis Hardley was born in a blitz-seiged Liverpool, in 1940. His teenage years were spent
doing odd jobs for the Beatles before becoming a Concorde engineer. In 1972, as an RAF
civilian, Dennis began photography, supplying pictures to *Scots Magazine*. In 1974, he moved
to Oban. Dennis has driven over 1,000,000 miles while photographing Scotland.

For my parents and for Joanna and Ginny
Lucinda Hawksley's love of Scotland was fed by childhood stories from grandparents of the
Monro and Ballantine clans. Although based in London, she takes frequent holidays in
Scotland and is a regular visitor to the Edinburgh Festival.
Picture on page 197 courtesy of the Bridgeman Art Library

With very grateful thanks to Helen Courtney, who designed this book, and to Sonya Newland

ISBN 1 84084 009 9

First published in 1998 by
DEMPSEY PARR
13 Whiteladies Road
Clifton Bristol BS8 1PB

Copyright 1998 © Dempsey Parr

Produced for Dempsey Parr by Foundry Design and Production,
The Long House, Antrobus Road, Chiswick, London W4 5HY.

THE MAGIC & MYSTERY OF
SCOTLAND

PHOTOGRAPHS BY DENNIS HARDLEY

Text by Lucinda Hawksley

DP
DEMPSEY
PARR

Contents

Contents by Region

Introduction

Anyone who has ever visited Scotland leaves with the burning desire to return. It is a mesmerising country whose landscape is imbued with a proud history and enriched by fantastic legends.

Scotland's major cities, Edinburgh and Glasgow, are similar in many ways to other large cities throughout the globe: international chains of shops; rucksack-clad, camera-toting tourists; rush-hour traffic jams and pavements teeming with busy people. However neither town, despite their size, number of inhabitants and international popularity, lose that essential quality of Scotchness. The bagpipe players at the corners of streets, the resonant snatches of accented conversations and the abundance of tartan are not just a lucrative facade with which to captivate tourists; all these things are still a genuine part of the Scotch heritage. Even at the pinnacle of the holiday season, or the bustle of a saturday afternoon's shopping, one need only glance upwards to view Edinburgh's majestic castle, or look around to see Charles Rennie Mackintosh's Glasgow School of Art, to know that the thin veneer of tourism can never suffocate the true, vibrant spirit of Scotland. Just as the Romans, Vikings and English could never subjugate the will of the Scottish people.

Scotland is, on an international scale, a relatively small country. Attached thickly at its southern borders to the north of England, the two are a world apart. Mainland Scotland has far more in common – a shared culture, history and way of thinking – with its detached, often far-flung islands, than it has with its southerly neighbour. In spite of this, Scotland is an intrinsic part of the United Kingdom, a political combination of the British Isles: Scotland, England, Northern Ireland and Wales. Until recently, the United Kingdom was ruled as one nation, however in 1997, the Scottish people voted in favour of devolution – a vote which has returned much of the country's decision-making powers to those whose lives the decisions affect.

Mainland Scotland covers 30,000 square miles, of which approximately 3,000 is islands: the Outer Hebrides, Inner Hebrides, Orkneys and Shetlands. These small swathes of Scotland contain some of the globe's most alluring landscapes and have revealed many of the ancient world's most fascinating secrets. The Industrial Revolution of the nineteenth century irrevocably changed the face of most small communities in the western world, however most of the Scottish isles still have a strong Gaelic-speaking community and retain values and lifestyles lost elsewhere.

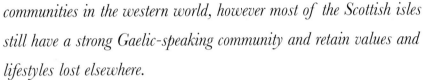

The great variety of peoples who have inhabited Scotland, attracted by fish-abundant waters, rich soil and lush vegetation, date back to the depths of pre-history. The islands have a particularly long history of habitation and here archaeological evidence has uncovered facets of Stone Age, Bronze Age, Iron Age and Neolithic cultures. For centuries Scotland was the most northerly part of civilised world, with early settlers arriving from France, Scandinavia and Spain as well as other parts of the British Isles, but the first truly Scottish peoples to feature in recorded history are the Picts.

The word 'Picts' means 'painted ones' and was the name first bestowed by their Roman invaders. In AD 43, the Roman Empire made its first attempt to colonise Britain. By AD 82 England and Wales had been annexed. It was at this time that the new rulers turned their attention to the land they called 'Caledonia', a so-far unconquerable country inhabited by fierce warrior tribes. The Picts and Celts — the races so fiercely opponent to the Roman invasion — called their country 'Alba'.

The Picts were so named because of their painted tribal marks, denoting a person's family background and social status. The Celts (whose name means 'kilted people') also practised body art, but favoured permanent tattooing. When the Romans arrived in Scotland, they found the Picts and Celts co-existing in a land rich with

empirical opportunity. They wrote many amused accounts of the painted and tattooed inhabitants of this new land and were impressed by their tribal cultures and warring abilities. However they remained utterly convinced that this new territory would eventually surrender.... In less than 150 years the Romans finally admitted defeat and returned to the sanctity of their flourishing – and subservient – empire. Scotland was left in peace.

In the fourth century, Scotland was taken over by a new, though benign, force from Rome. Christianity. In 397 St Ninian, a local man who returned from travelling in Italy, built Scotland's first church at Whithorn, in Wigtown Bay. In 563, St Columba arrived on the shores of Iona; an exile from his native Ireland. He was a charismatic, forward-thinking man whose following rapidly flourished. He spoke Gaelic, the same tongue as the Celts – a throwback to the time when Ireland was joined to the rest of Britain; he also became allied with the Pictish community by visiting their king in a gesture of peace. This remarkable saint shaped the consciousness of Scotland and recreated the course of history.

The history of the Celts is a well-documented one; they assimilated Columba's faith into their culture and are the ancestors of today's people of Scotland. However the fate of their Pictish counterparts is a mystery to this day. In spite of their prominence in early recorded history, the extinction of their race and culture remains an untold story. The first records of their existence date back to AD 297 and it is known that, unlike the Celts, they spoke a non-Indo-European tongue, which eventually merged with a form of Celtic language. To this day, the Picts' country of origin and their final fate remains a mystery.

Having vanquished their Roman army, the people of Scotland were destined never to be free from invasion. In ensuing centuries they suffered continual attacks from Scandinavia, often losing portions of their land to the Norsemen. In more recent centuries, the Scots' greatest enemy has been their English neighbours. The Borders were a constant victim in the repetitive warfare, just as the Orkneys and Shetland Islands suffered from the Viking raiders. In 1603, James VI of Scotland, a Stuart, became James I of England thus joining the two countries. This did not end the English-Scotch hostilities, instead the battle for supremacy was only just beginning.

Over the next few centuries the majority of Scots were poor farm labourers or 'crofters', an easy prey for the injustices of their lairds – landowners who were either English or unconcerned wealthy Scots often living far from their properties. Matters came to a head after the potato famine (concurrent with that in Ireland) and 'the Clearances' of the nineteenth century. Many devastated families left to seek new lives in New Zealand, Australia and North America, but those who stayed began to fight back. Finally the national newspapers took up their cause, the government took notice and an act of parliament was passed. The plight of the crofters was vastly improved. Since then Scotland has made many steps towards independence.

The landscapes and beauty of Scotland are renowned throughout the world. mention the word 'Scotland' and mental images of ruined castles, mist-shrouded mountains, shining lochs, heather-covered moors and russet highland cattle will appear. Reminiscences of whisky-warmed evenings beside a cosy pub fire, New Year's Day shinty matches blowing away the cobwebs of an over-indulgent Hogmanay, or balmy summer nights watching an Edinburgh street performer spill to the fore of conversation. Everyone who has been here will come back one day.

THE MAGIC & MYSTERY OF SCOTLAND

LANDSCAPES & SEASCAPES

Scotland is a land of breathtaking landscapes and dramatic seascapes; sumptuous views of bloom-covered moors, luxuriant golden beaches and vivid images of distant islands lit by a setting sun.

View to Jura from Gigha
ARGYLLSHIRE

The peaceful Isle of Jura can be seen here from the north-west coast of Gigha, looking out over a smoothly rippled sea of purest sky-blue. Both Gigha and Jura derive their names from the Norse language: 'jura' means 'deer island' and 'gigha' means 'God's island'. On both islands can be found standing stones and burial cairns dating back in history to long before the Celts or Norsemen arrived.

In keeping with its name, Jura currently has a deer population of around 6500; in stark contrast to its human population of around 200. Measuring twenty-eight miles by eight miles, Jura is larger than a great many Scots islands; however much of it is uninhabitable. It is spliced almost in two by the great fault that became Loch Tarbert, to the south of which, lie the Paps of Jura. Individually, the mountains are named: 'An Oir', 'The Mountain of Gold'; 'Shiantiadh', 'The Holy Mountain' and 'A Chaolais', 'The Mountain of the Sound'.

Jura has several claims to fame: St Earnan, uncle of St Columba, is buried here; so is Mary MacCrain who apparently lived to the grand age of 128. The island also has a more modern tale of fame: in the 1940s, George Orwell stayed here to write *1984*.

Evening sky over Connel
ARGYLLSHIRE

The small village of Connel and the gentle slopes of the hills of Mull are lit spectacularly in the outstanding colours of a burnished evening sky. The perfectly reflected, almost mirror images, of the boats draw attention to the stillness of the loch – not a single puff of breeze, nor movement from a bow so much as undulates the water's surface. Out of sight are the planes, the trains and the ships of the twentieth century, but in Connel there is a scene which, otherwise, could so easily be part of another era.

Connel itself is perhaps most famous for its bridge, a replica of the Forth Bridge, sited at the more southerly Firth of Forth. Connel Bridge provides a safe crossing and superb viewpoint over the Falls of Lora, a tempestuous conglomeration of currents and tides, mingling the waters from Loch Linnhe, Loch Etive, the Firth of Lorne and the Sound of Mull. It is the only seawater falls anywhere in Europe and the sight is spectacular.

Isles of Rhum and Eigg from Morar

ARGYLLSHIRE

This idyllic picture shows the Inner Hebridean islands of Rhum and Eigg, as seen from the shores of Morar.

Rhum, which was created from a long-extinct volcano, is considerably larger than Eigg, whose entire surface covers only about thirteen square miles. For centuries Rhum was inhabited by crofters, but since the Clearances, has remained almost deserted. Today it is a national park, home to many undisturbed deer.

Eigg nestles comfortably beneath Rhum's south shore. To its south is the tiny island of Muck and to the east lies the mainland. It is from the east that this view can be seen.

The peaceful sands of Morar, with indolent boats resting amongst the dunes, evoke an image of lives spent in contentment, yet Morar and

its loch, which reaches the phenomenal depth of up to 1000ft, once witnessed a feverish manhunt. An island in the loch's centre was the hiding place of Lord Lovat, an English aristocrat and spy – who had been informing on both sides in the Jacobite uprisings. In June 1746, he was captured by the Hanoverian troops, forcibly removed to London and beneaded.

The River Tay from Kinnoull Hill
PERTH PERTHSHIRE

Kinnoull Hill in Perth, East Scotland, rises to 729ft above the city. From its summit the majestic River Tay, spectacularly blue in image here, can be seen to stretch for miles before feeding into Loch Tay: a 14-mile-long body of water that reaches depths of over 500ft. Before *c.*1452, Perth was Scotland's capital city and as such its river would have seen a profusion of important activity: as a route for traders, irrigation for the crops, and the main water supply for the people. It winds from Perth, through Scone, Birnam and Aberfeldy into Loch Tay.

Perhaps the most famous of the Tay's landmarks is that of Birnam Wood, immortalised in William Shakespeare's *Macbeth*. Little remains of the great wood today, but one oak, the 'Birnam Oak' still stands alongside the Tay and is said to have been there since the time of Macbeth, who reigned from 1040–57.

The tower seen here is Kinnoull Tower, an eighteenth-century edifice built by the ninth Earl of Kinnoull. While travelling through Germany, the Earl was so impressed by the elegant towers on the banks of the Rhine, that he determined to build his own replicas on his return to Scotland.

General Wade's Bridge
ABERFELDY PERTHSHIRE

This bridge across Perthshire's River Tay, was built by George Wade (1673–1748). An English Major-General, Wade was sent to Scotland for the first time in 1724. His orders were to create a decent road system, including bridge building, to increase Scotland's accessibility – for the English militia.

In 1725, Wade was also given orders to disarm the Highlanders; he is remembered for doing so with diplomacy and with the aid of clansmen he had befriended. He was memorably deceived by the Jacobite forces behind Bonnie Prince Charlie, who tricked General Wade's platoon into believing that the prince's troops had retreated, during the upsurgence of the Forty-Five. In retribution, Wade was prominent among those who defeated the Jacobites in 1746.

Between 1724 and 1736, General Wade built 250 miles of modern road. As can be seen from this photograph, his structures were sturdy and have withstood the test of time. The following lines were written after the end of his campaign:

Had you seen these roads
before they were made,
You would lift up your hands
and bless General Wade.

Towards Cuillin Hills from Loch Slapin
SKYE INNER HEBRIDES

This scene is one of extraordinary beauty. The contrast of the vivid-green of algae-covered boulders with a biscuit-coloured sand, steely granite mountains and the tantalisingly clear blue of the sky, also reflected in the water, is visual perfection.

Cuillin Hills at Blaven are sited at the shore of Skye's Loch Slapin. Black Cuillin, the largest and most formidable of the jagged range of hills, houses Loch Coruisk, one of the least accessible and most mysterious lochs in Scotland: it is often inhabited by colonies of seals delighting in their private swimming pool.

Skye has long been renowned for its inspirational atmosphere, and many writers and artists have spent time on the island, patiently waiting for the muse of Skye to help with the creation of masterpieces. One of the island's greatest native poets was Mairi Mh'r nan Oran. She was a staunch protester against the injustices of landowners towards their Celtic tenants and wrote many verses of protest that have retained their angry sting of injustice.

Beach on Iona
INNER HEBRIDES

Iona is a tiny island, just one mile wide and three-and-a-half miles long. It has a thirteenth-century nunnery with a carefully tended, peaceful garden; an abbey created from pink stone; a shrine to the sixth-century St Columba; an eleventh-century chapel dedicated to St Oran and a thriving Gaelic-speaking community. At one time Iona was also known for its smooth, cooling green stone known as Iona Marble, which was quarried in large quantities – a practice which has now been stopped for environmental reasons.

The pink-stone abbey, at one time the very pinnacle of the Celtic Christian world, was closely allied with Ireland's equally important Mayo Abbey; to this day both places retain a strong link to the evocative mystique of their pasts. The island of Iona is known in legend throughout the world. People who have never visited Scotland, who barely know where it is on the map, associate the very word 'Iona' with spirituality. It was centuries ago that Iona was St Columba's famed seat of Christianity, but somehow the essence of such fervour remains imprinted in the very letters of its name.

Atlantic breakers on the Isle of Barra
OUTER HEBRIDES

Forceful waves slapping against the rocky outcrops of Barra's west coast, present a powerful image of the Outer Hebridean island. Barra is a picturesque island dripping in history: from its Iron Age broch at Dun Chuidhir or the eleventh-century Kisimul Castle, stronghold of the Clan McLeod; the Neolithic burial cairn at Dun Bharpa to the nineteenth-century fishing port of Castlebay, wherever one walks on the island seems to lead to another era.

At Vatersay Bay is a monument to honour the dead of a shipwreck that occurred in the nineteenth century. As is often the case with the seas around Scotland, the waves around Barra can swell to angry heights and the sea-bed is a maze of cripplingly sharp rocks. In 1853, the *Annie Jane* left Liverpool, laden with hundreds of emigrants intent on swapping a harsh life of urban poverty for an imagined glorious future in Canada. A furious sea grew to massive proportions and the ship was tossed about wildly before lurching on to the rocks at Vatersay. Almost all the passengers were drowned.

Rhum from Moidart
ARDNAMURCHAN PENINSULA ARGYLLSHIRE

This dramatic view towards the Inner Hebridean island of Rhum, is seen from the shore of mainland Scotland, at the Ardnamurchan Peninsula. It is the most westerly point in mainland Britain and, therefore, the last place the sun sets. The name 'Ardnamurchan' is Gaelic and translates into English as 'Point of the Great Ocean'.

All along the craggy shore of Moidart, the islands of Rhum and Eigg are visible on a clear day. There is a loch in this area, Loch Moidart, from which, when the tide is high, rises an island; when the tide is low, the islet can be seen to be joined to the shore. At low tide it is possible to walk from the loch's banks to one of the ancient seats of the Clan MacDonald.

At Kinlochmoidart, not far from where this picture was taken, are seven beech trees, standing alone in commemoration. They were planted in memory of the seven men who accompanied Bonnie Prince Charlie from France at the start of the Jacobite uprising. It was here that the prince and his men first landed on his return to Scotland's shores.

Bluebell Wood near Benderloch
ARGYLLSHIRE

The word 'Argyll' comes from the Gaelic language and means 'Coast of the Gaels'. It was sometime around the fifth century AD, that Gaelic-speaking people arrived from Ireland and settled in the area now known as Argyll – a large stretch of Scottish land, with a diverse range of scenery: craggy coastline, seemingly bottomless lochs, remote moorland, undulating hills and acres and acres of woodland. This photograph was taken in woods close to the small village of Benderloch. The camera has captured a perfect moment: a clear, white sky can be seen through elegant trees; on the ground spreads a carpet of bluebells, looking as purple as heather in the shadow of the trunks; to the left-hand side, the vivid green of a Scots hillside is visible.

Scotland is renowned for the abundance of its plants and flowers. Despite the cold weather usually associated with this part of the world, the west and north coasts of Scotland play host to the Gulf Stream, a warm front of air which travels from the Gulf of Mexico. This diversity in temperature means that Scotland's climate is ideal for wildflowers – it is said that eighty per cent of all the world's plants would be able to survive, and thrive, in Scotland.

Beach near Crossapoll
TIREE INNER HEBRIDES

The Isle of Tiree is a place of beauty and tradition. A strong Gaelic-speaking community retains steadfast links with its past, when Tiree was a land of crofters. One explanation of the word 'tiree' is that it comes from the Gaelic words *tir-lodh* which mean 'land of the corn'; though sadly Tiree's days of agricultural splendour were largely ended by the Clearances. The island, at ten miles long and up to four miles wide, is now home to roughly 850 people – a drastic reduction of the former crofting population of 4500.

Another explanation of the island's name is that it means 'land lower than the waves', a fitting title, indicative of Tiree's flat landscape.

The Edinburgh writer, Sir Walter Scott, visited Tiree in the company of the talented engineer and lighthouse builder Robert Stevenson (the grandfather of writer Robert Louis Stevenson). After his trip, Scott wrote this eulogy to Scotland's wondrous scenery,

Caledonia ...
... Land of brown heath and shaggy wood
Land of the mountain and the flood.

Sir Walter Scott

Sunset Over Harris
OUTER HEBRIDES

This idyllic image of the sun setting behind a mountain on Harris captures the natural splendour of the remote community. Harris is actually attached by a swathe of land to the Isle of Lewis, but each retains distinct island communities. The landscape of Harris is one of diversity, there are mountains in the north, with summits stretching up to and above 2000ft; in the east are fjords and in the west are beaches of blindingly white sand.

South Harris is home to the evocatively named Golden Road. There are two versions of the story as to how the road came by its name: one is that the sun, reflected from the lochs' surfaces, make the road ahead appear paved with gold; the other is that the road cost so much to build. Also in the south is the village of Rodel, formerly the island's capital and a thriving port, town and religious centre. Sited here is the fifteenth-century St Clement's church, the burial place of the Clan McLeod and home to the wonderfully egotistical tomb of Alisdair Crotach, eighth chief of the McLeods of Dunvegan. He commissioned a funereal carving in 1528 – nineteen years before his death. The sculpture is covered with scenes of Crotach's life and of his soul being greeted by biblical figures.

Arnprior
THE TROSSACHS STIRLING REGION

The dramatic evening light seen here colouring the hay field and houses of the village of Arnprior has an almost ethereal glow. Arnprior is in the Trossachs, a place of outstanding scenery that joins two great lochs: Loch Achray and Loch Katrine. 'The Trossachs' literally means 'the Bristly Country', an apt description of a ruggedly diverse area filled with trees and shrubs and coated liberally with that quintessential Scotch flora, heather.

Sir Walter Scott, to whom this area was well known, used the area around Loch Katrine for much of the setting of his novel *Rob Roy*. He mentions 'the goblins' cave' (Coire nan Uruisgean), where Rob Roy and his band hid their stolen cattle. He also offered an explanation of Loch Katrine's derivation. The lake is not, as one might suppose, named after a woman, its name is actually a corruption of the word 'caterans', a local term for 'pirates'. Centuries ago, there were a great many pirates who made use of Scotland's numerous interlocking waterways, Loch Katrine was a favourite meeting point.

Salen
LISMORE ARGYLLSHIRE

The Isle of Lismore was once the most important religious seat throughout the whole Gaelic-speaking world. It was home to the ancient seat of the revered bishopric of Argyll – active and dominant from the thirteenth to the sixteenth centuries – and housed the beautifully illuminated *Book of the Dean of Lismore;* a collection of Gaelic and English medieval poems. Many other examples of fine Celtic artistry have also been uncovered at Lismore, including spectacular metal work.

Today Lismore is a tranquil, green island with a small population. The island's extent is ten miles in length and just one-and-a-half miles at its widest part. Despite its small size, it is also host to two castles, albeit now in ruins, and the remains of an Iron Age settlement, or 'broch'.

In its heyday, Lismore and its community maintained strong links with Ireland, another Gaelic-speaking centre of early Christianity. Much of Lismore's history and depth of religious feeling can still be felt, retained in the stones of the island and the legacy of its early settlers.

Arinagour Harbour
COLL INNER HEBRIDES

Arinagour is the main town, the harbour and ferry port of Coll – a world away from the bustling harbours of cities such as Aberdeen or Inverness. The relaxed, Inner Hebridean island is a place of peace; spread over a landmass of roughly forty square miles.

Coll was once a crofting community, a population which was decimated by the Clearances and the potato famine, as were the inhabitants of neighbouring Tiree; nowadays, Coll is home to around 150 people and the gentle lowing of dairy herds.

Small though the island is, communities throughout history have left their mark. As well as the empty crofts, there are Iron Age settlements, ancient crannogs (Celtic lochside huts) and a medieval cemetery. At the summit of the island's highest hill, is a large, immovable boulder, believed to have been transported there during earth fluctuations in the Ice Age.

On lower ground, to the west of the island, are two magnificent standing stones. They are named *Na Sgeulachan* or 'tellers of tales'. Their purpose is uncertain, though two possible explanations have been offered: that they are part of a now ruined temple, or perhaps were used as some kind of astrological calendar.

Loch Lurgainn and Stac Polly
INVERNESS-SHIRE

From behind the wind-ruffled waters of Loch Lurgainn can be seen the illustrious slopes of Stac Polly (also called *Stac Pollaidh*) from whose instantly recognisable summit, fantastic views of the north can be seen. Stac Polly rises to 2900ft out of a protected area: the Inverapolly National Nature Reserve. As a result, the ground at the mountain's foot remains naturally plant-ed, lush and unspoilt. The rugged power of mountains and bitterly cold depths of lochs create a stunning, almost frightening contrast; there are few landscapes that can make one feel so utterly-mortal as this conjunction of unseen depth and overwhelming height.

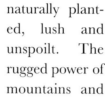

In the foreground of the photograph bursts a profusion of purple heather, one of the Highland's most famous sym-bols. Throughout August and September, heather decorates the mountains in a luxurious array of blooms, a spectacular sight when considering that there are over three million acres of heather moors throughout Scotland.

Heather has become a vital part of Scotch life, and is used in so many and diverse ways: for thatching roofs; for firewood; to make rope, brooms and baskets; and for making heather wine, honey and that most Scotch of all products – heather whisky.

Hump-back Bridge
GLEN KINGLAS ARGYLLSHIRE

The stone hump-back bridge in Glen Kinglas, crosses the icy waters of a stream near Cairndow, south-east of Loch Fyne. The area has long been a popular place for holiday makers and, in 1803, Dorothy and William Wordsworth were among those who travelled the ancient road on horseback. The scenery inspired the poet to write several sonnets about Scotland.

An old pass meanders its way through the glen, a track often trodden by soldiers in centuries past. It is a difficult track, exhausting to climb, steeply winding and sometimes fatal to travellers. After a laborious ascent, the climber comes across the aptly named Rest-and-be-thankful – a place so-titled after an inscribed stone that bears those words.

A few miles away from this snow-covered bridge can be found St Columba's Cave. It is believed that the saint arrived in Scotland near the site of the cave and used its shelter to hold Christian ceremonies. Within its depths are an altar shelf, replete with carved crosses, there is also a basin-like dip that the saint reputedly used as a baptismal font.

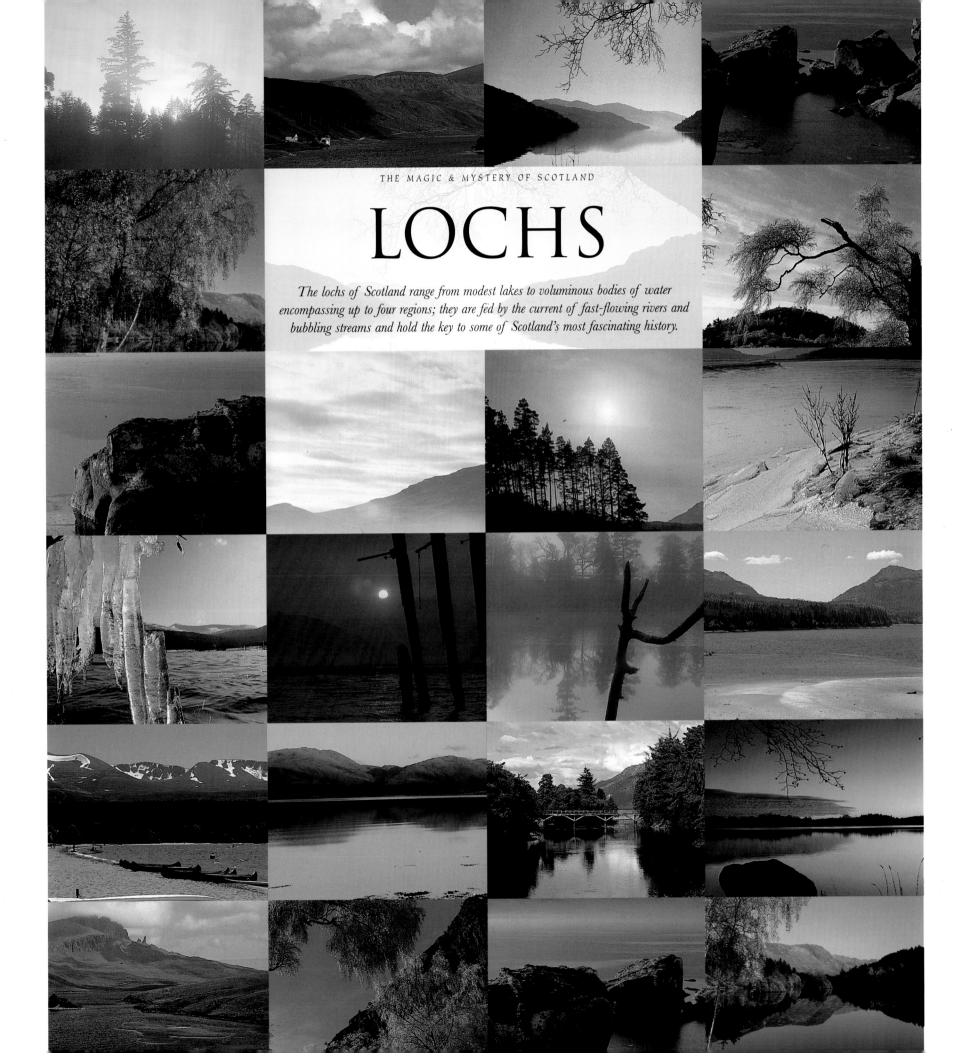

LOCHS

The lochs of Scotland range from modest lakes to voluminous bodies of water encompassing up to four regions; they are fed by the current of fast-flowing rivers and bubbling streams and hold the key to some of Scotland's most fascinating history.

Loch Ba
RANNOCH MOOR PERTHSHIRE

Perthshire's stunning Loch Ba, is seen here from the shore on a misty morning. Loch Ba is near Rannoch Moor, an area of cleared land, which once formed part of the ancient Caledonian Forest; it was also the base and hiding place of both William Wallace and Robert the Bruce. The wildness of the area made it an impossibility for non-native soldiers to search successfully; only those who knew the area inside out, such as Bruce and Wallace, could hope the conquer it. With forbidding mountains, desolate landscape and enveloping peat bogs, Rannoch Moor was a treacherous place for strangers.

There are tales of spirits who haunt the moor: water kelpies from the lochs and fairies from the woodland. There are also stories of monsters and ghostly animals, such as dogs and horses. This photograph, with its shrouded islet and single, defiant tree, make the myths appear plausible. If Loch Ness has a secret resident, it seems equally likely that Loch Ba could contain one too.

Loch Laggan
from the Frozen Shore
LAGGAN INVERNESS-SHIRE

When biting Boreas, fell and doure,
Sharp shivers thro' the leafless bow'r;
When Phoebus gies a short-liv'd glow'r,
Far south the lift,
Dim-dark'ning thro' the flaky show'r,
Or whirling drift.

Robert Burns

Robbie Burns' poem, 'A Winter Night', describes just such a sunset as this view over Loch Laggan.

Inverness-shire, in the heart of the Scottish Highlands, is home to many clans; a warrior people whose need to survive the harsh winters of their homeland made them strong, fearsome opponents in battle. Just a few miles from Loch Laggan, an incredible eighteenth-century victory was won by the MacDonalds of Keppoch. Their territory was being invaded by a swarm of Hanoverian soldiers, working their way from Fort Augustus to Fort William. With a vengeful battle cry, a formation of naked Highlanders descended on the scores of soldiers. Although far superior in numbers, the English turned and fled – routed by just twelve furious clansmen.

Highland Loch in Winter
HIGHLAND REGION

Icy stalactites hang from lochside shrubs at the end of a Highland winter; the unfrozen loch suggesting a tentative start of spring. Spring in the Highlands is a unique experience, the time when new, green heather buds are appearing on the hillsides; when young red deer can be seen in the hills, and when Highland Cattle can be seen without the mournful backdrop of snow-covered grass.

The Highlands are prolific in history and tradition. When Roman invaders took control of England, they were unable to penetrate into Scotland, because of the force of the Caledonian warriors. Today this proud history has been kept alive through Highland dress, Highland games and Highland dancing. Highland dancing is reflective of a Celtic form of worship, as a celebration of nature's forces, paying homage to the sun or the crops. Highland dress is a tradition that started way back in the sands of time; although most people associate Scots with the formal, pleated kilt it is in fact a nineteenth-century invention, attributed to the novelist Sir Walter Scott. After the Battle of Culloden, it was made illegal to wear Highland dress, but Scott re-introduced it back into society, in the form of the stylised kilt, during a visit to Edinburgh by the King.

Loch Linnhe
BALLACHULISH ARGYLLSHIRE

Argyllshire's Loch Linnhe is seen here from the old pier at south Ballachulish. For almost three centuries, Ballachulish was famed for its slate quarries, the old pier was used to move the slate onto boats for export. Sadly the works were closed down in 1955. Capturing the mood in a fiercely red sunset, Dennis Hardley has encapsulated the poignancy of the town's lost industry, a loss marked by the pier's crumbling remains.

Not far from Loch Linnhe is the village of Onich, a place which derives its name from its nearby loch. *Onich* is a Gaelic word that translates to 'white shore', a picturesque description of the waves that rear up from a wind-angered lake.

Ballachulish Bridge is the notorious site of the execution of an innocent.

James Stewart, or 'James of the Glens', was falsely hanged by the Clan Campbell, in a blood-chilling exaction of revenge for the murder of one of their number. The true murderer was never found, so a scape-goat was found, tried and robbed of his life to give the Campbell's vengeance. At the site of James Stewart's execution is a white memorial stone mourning the death of an innocent man.

Winter Reflections on Loch Fyne
ARGYLLSHIRE

This clear reflection of a sunset-lit Loch Fyne captures the view towards the tiny village of Inverary. Loch Fyne is an elongated stretch of lake that rounds the north shore of the Cowal Peninsula, feeding, eventually, into the Firth of Clyde and the water that surrounds the Inner Hebridean islands of Bute, Cumbrae, Little Cumbrae and Arran.

A few miles from Inverary is a love token, a historical marker of a time long gone. The marker is in the shape of a heart, created by careful placing of smooth stones; it was the traditional wedding spot for travelling gypsies when passing through Argyllshire.

Argyllshire was the first port of call for refugees leaving Ireland to start a new life in Scotland. After the arrival of St Columba in the sixth century, an exodus of Irish Christians occurred, following in the footsteps of their revered leader. It was to the shores of this area of Scotland that these first pilgrims came, bringing with them, it has long been reputed, the Stone of Destiny, better known as the Stone of Scone.

Sunset over Loch Awe
ARGYLLSHIRE

This spectacular view takes the eye over a silent Loch Awe in the glow of a misty sunset. The perfect reflections of the driftwood and framing avenue of trees, convey an atmosphere of absolute stillness, not even so much as a breath of breeze ruffles the water's surface.

Loch Awe is one of the Highland's most impressive bodies of water, its long, slim frame housing several islets, a medieval church and the ancient burial ground of the Clan Macarthur. There are also two ruined castles: one, Kilchurn Castle, is the seat of the Clan Campbell; the other is the seat of the Clan Macnaughton.

The first mention of Loch Awe in history is in a charter dated 1267: in it, the then King, Alexander III (1249–86), is depicted handing his own castle, on the shores of Loch Awe, to the Macnaughton family. The charter lays down the condition that the clan should be available and willing to supply military protection for the castle, also that they should ensure the king hospitality in their new home, whenever he demanded it.

Loch Laggan
LAGGAN INVERNESS-SHIRE

The breathtaking luminescence captured in this image of Loch Laggan shows the incredible array of colours which make up a Scots summer. This warm scene is in stark comparison to the earlier view of the same loch in a snow-biting winter. Scotland is a country of vivid contrasts and the countryside around Loch Laggan can be as bleak and terrifying in winter as it is lush and welcoming in summer.

This body of water is surrounded by rugged moorland and overbearing mountains, some of which reach upwards of 3000ft. Throughout this area there are many lakes, all linked by a series of intricate tunnels, running both overland and beneath the mountains. Loch Laggan connects with two other lochs: Treig and Moy. Over the years, the combined waters of the lochs have been tamed and trained by industry to spill into the depths of Ben Nevis and out to the aluminium works on the other side of the mountain.

Loch Morlich
GLEN MORE INVERNESS-SHIRE

A peaceful view of Loch Morlich's beach illustrates a typical scene at the shore of this picturesque loch. The weather conditions around this part of Scotland, make Loch Morlich the ideal place for watersports, and windsurfers can often be seen brightly skimming the water's surface – and almost as often falling into it.

The mountain backdrop to this colourful view shows the Cairngorm mountains; a range which stretches for miles between Aviemore and Braemar. The highest of these mountains is Cairn Gorm itself, with a summit which measures up to 4048ft; of all the other mountains in the range, there are fifty whose tips reach over 3000ft. The name *cairn gorm* translates to 'blue mountain' and has given the mountain range its anglicised name; the expression is attributed to the mountain's peak which looks blue when viewed from a distance. However the Gaelic name of the range is actually *Arn Monadh Ruadh* and means 'the red hills', a name which derives from the pink granite found on the range's plateaux.

Winter Frost on the shore of Loch Etive
ARGYLLSHIRE

The visual impact of this dusk scene is tremendous: the pewter-coloured boulders at the lake's edge, combine with the orange-pink of a winter sunset to create an image which has captured the true essence of photography – the desire to encapsulate a perfect fragment of time.

Loch Etive is fed by the running freshwater of the River Awe, in turn the loch empties its overflowing waters into the saltwater rush at Connel, mingling with the flow of waters from Loch Linnhe, the Firth of Lorne and the Sound of Mull. It is this coming together of various gentle bodies of water that creates the turbulent Falls of Lora.

Etive is a picturesque loch slicing through the heart of the lonely Glen Etive, a valley that looks down to the chilling depths of Glencoe. From its shores, Ben Cruachan can be seen. The mountain contains a reservoir of water, held high up on a dipped plateau of the mountain. This reservoir is used to power the Cruachan Power Station, a hydro-electric power plant that supplies electricity to all the surrounding villages.

Loch Ness
INVERNESS-SHIRE

Loch Ness lies within the Great Glen, a 300-million-year-old fault in the earth's crust which stretches from Inverness to Fort William, shaped by the ravages of the ice ages. It is 24 miles long, one mile wide with a bed at depths of up to 700ft. One of the most remarkable attributes of Loch Ness is that, throughout recorded history, it has never been known to freeze.

The first mention of a monster in Loch Ness comes from the sixth century: when St Columba first arrived in Scotland, one of his monks is reported to have disturbed a monster while swimming in the loch. The saint pacified the angry beast, by making the sign of the cross and telling it to return to the water. From then on, there were no more reports, until the 1930s. Many people have claimed to see the fabled Nessie and images have been captured on film – none of which has proved conclusive. Occasional hoaxes have grabbed press attention, but while Nessie's existence has never been proved, neither has the loch been proved empty. One can only hope that the mystery of Loch Ness will remain a secret forever, and that, whatever it is that lurks there, will be allowed to exist in peace.

Lake of Menteith
THE TROSSACHS STIRLING REGION

A spectacular sunset silhouettes the landscape at the shore of the Lake of Menteith, a lake on which resides an island known as the Isle of Rest. The island is famed for its ruins of the once stately Inchmaholm Priory. The monks who inhabited the building in its days of prosperity, were farmers. They grew vegetables to feed themselves, but also raised sheep, becoming wool farmers to raise money to pay for their supplies.

The priory dates back to the thirteenth century and was an important hub of monastic life until the Reformation in the sixteenth century. After the religious upheaval that heralded the death of so many monastic communities, Inchmaholm Priory was given, by the government, to John Erskine, seventh Earl of Mar in return for his services as Royal Treasurer.

At this time, most of the land around the Lake of Menteith was bogland, a dangerous, unfarmable and uninhabitable swamp. This was all to change at the end of the eighteenth century with the attentions of the distinguished lawyer and keen agriculturist Lord Henry Kames. The peer imported an enormous water-wheel to drain the treacherous bogs, yielding acres of eminently cultivable land, and some of the richest soil in the Stirling Region.

Shore of Loch Assynt
SUTHERLAND

This atmospheric scene at the shore of a reflective Loch Assynt, is seen from a point near the village of Lochinver. In the distance can be seen the mountain of Suilven, also known as 'the Matterhorn of Scotland', a noble formation with a height of 2399ft. Suilven is part of the Inverapolly Nature Reserve, a landscape it shares with Stac Polly, Cul Mor, Cul Beag and Canisp. Suilven is the smallest mountain in the range, but distinctive by its unusual shape; a shape which has earned the mountain the nickname of 'the sugar loaf'.

Loch Assynt has become an area of great interest to geologists and there are often international geologists studying the rocks around the loch. Part of Sutherland and bordering Caithness is known as the Flow Country, an area of bogland concealing a rich history. Enveloped in the marshes (the word 'flow' comes from 'floi', the Norse word for 'marsh') can be found ancient plant remains, fossilised into peat and dating back to *c.* 5000 BC.

Loch Assynt in Winter
SUTHERLAND

Loch Assynt, seen here with a beautifully mesmeric frame of laced ice, is located in Sutherland, at Scotland's north-west corner. Sutherland is an area of diverse landscapes, rich in beauty, but also one of Scotland's most inhospitable terrains: wild cliffs, lonely moorland, forbidding mountains, deep lochs and deserted beaches.

This area has long been the focus of scientific research: the remains of many prehistoric life forms have been found in caves and other dwellings around the shores of Loch Assynt. Close by, a memorial stone tells the story of Peach and Horne, two eminent geologists of the nineteenth century, who made the researching of this area their lifes' work.

There is history at almost every turn in the county: crumbling castles, medieval churches, ancient mills, ruined Iron Age settlements; there are even echoes of the ill-fated Sutherland 'gold rush' of the late nineteenth century. Sutherland was also home to the last witch-burning in Scotland, a macabre event that took place in 1722.

A Lochan near Glencoe
ARGYLLSHIRE

This autumnal view of a still lochan shows the hills around Kinlochleven in perfect reflection. This peaceful scenery poignantly belies the echoes of Scotland's most treacherous blood bath, which took place at nearby Glencoe. A massacre of Scots, by fellow Scots, under the orders of their own government. The MacDonalds had refused to swear allegiance to the new usurper of the throne and, as a result, the clan's obliteration was desired and ordered.

The Clan Campbell spent two weeks as guests of the hospitable, and trusting, MacDonald clan, when, in the dead of night on 13 February 1692, the deceitful guests surprised and brutally murdered thirty-eight of the two-hundred-strong MacDonalds. Their orders were to eradicate the entire clan, but fortunately snow and severe storms prevented the Campbell soldiers from blocking the MacDonalds' escape routes, as planned – although the fierce weather also meant that many more of the already-butchered clan perished while escaping. The echoes of the bloody act and the terrified, frantic flight of the MacDonald survivors still seem locked in the air around Glencoe to this day.

Lochan Ovie
BADENOCH HIGHLAND REGION

This frosted scenery on the shore of Lochan Ovie is a glorious depiction of a Scottish autumn. The view can be seen to the south of Newtonmore, the birthplace of 'shinty' – the sport of the Highlands and Scotland's national pastime. Shinty is an ancient game, one of the oldest in the world; written reports of matches have been found dating back to the fourteenth century. To those who have never seen a shinty game, it is perhaps best described as similar to hockey: shinty teams are made up of twelve players, each carrying a curved stick or 'caman'; the aim is to gain control of the ball and score as many goals as possible in a ninety minute match. Traditionally, shinty matches are played at the start of January to herald in the New Year.

Lochan Ovie is in Badenoch, in the heart of the Highlands. It is an area famed for its most notorious son, Alexander Stewart, known as 'The Wolf of Badenoch'. From an island in the middle of Loch-an-Eilean he maintained a stronghold during his reign of terror. His barbaric acts, the most notorious being the burning of Elgin Cathedral, after its Bishop reprimanded him for deserting his wife, inspired fear in the hearts of all around him.

Loch Fada and Storr Rock
TROTTERNISH SKYE INNER HEBRIDES

The Trotternish peninsula is an oval-shaped mass of land, encompassing a wonderful rocky wilderness; a walkers' paradise and once the prime hiding place for the booty of cattle-rustlers. Stolen herds could be hidden here for years without fear of discovery.

The Trotternish Ridge is a spectacular spine of rock running from the island's rim to the Storr, a treacherous cliff with a fall of 2360ft into the foaming water below. Beneath the Storr itself, stands The Old Man of Storr, an illustrious black monolith of incredible height – from base to tip it measures over 160ft. At one time there were two rocks standing here, said to be the old man and his wife.

The smaller of the two, the wife, is no longer standing. There are many legends surrounding the couple who were turned to stone, including tales of giants who used to roam the earth and could turn a person to stone by looking at them.

Skye is perhaps best known as the place to which Bonnie Prince Charlie made his escape, dressed in women's clothing and posing as Flora MacDonald's maid. This famous escape inspired many songs, including the haunting 'Over the Sea to Skye'.

Loch Lomond
ARDLUI ARGYLLSHIRE

The tranquil, incredibly beautiful body of water that is Loch Lomond stretches on for twenty-four miles; varying in width from five miles to under one mile: it is the largest body of inland water throughout the whole of Britain. The south tip of the magnificent loch is in the lowlands – at an area sited about half an hour's drive north-east of the city of Glasgow – whereas the loch's north end flows into the rugged, domineering Highlands. When rowing on its waters, one is dwarfed by mountains; passing the majesty of Ben Vorlich and skirting the foot of the commanding Ben Lomond.

At the Highland end of the water, near Inversnaid, is 'Rob Roy's cave' – once the hideout of Scotland's favourite brigand and his clan. Robert Roy MacGregor was born in the Loch Lomond district and spent his outlawed years hiding in the accommodating mountains, until his death in 1734. He was immortalised in Sir Walter Scott's novel *Rob Roy* and has remained synonymous with Scottish folklore ever since. His grave can be found at Balquhidder, near Stirling. Rob Roy's cave and its surrounding crevices also have an earlier claim to fame: in 1306, centuries before the birth of the famous MacGregor, Robert the Bruce is believed to have hidden himself within the rocks.

51

GLENS & MOUNTAINS

The glens and mountains of Scotland are its most defining features; home to the country's largest animals, such as deer and Highland Cattle, as well as myriad birds, small animals and lustrous flowers.

The Three Sisters
PASS OF GLENCOE ARGYLLSHIRE

Argyllshire's Three Sisters are awe-inspiring, rugged mountains whose slopes are treacherous and have witnessed the death of many an inexperienced climber. Here they are seen from the pass of Glencoe. Within the slopes of the Three Sisters is a fissure in the rock surface, this is known as Ossian's Cave and is reputed to be the birthplace of the third-century Celtic bard. The poems of Ossian were translated into English by the eighteenth-century poet James Macpherson, although many critics disputed the so-called 'Ossianic' poems, believing instead that James Macpherson had written them himself.

The Three Sisters look down to Glencoe, a lush glen with a bloody past. This is the place where, on 13 February of each year, a group of MacDonalds meet to remember the massacre of their ancestors by the treacherous Clan Campbell in 1692. Inside the glen is a slender Celtic cross, carved in stone and set upon a small mound. It is dedicated to Maclain, chief of the Glencoe Clan MacDonald who perished in the massacre of his people.

Ben Cruachan from Loch Etive
CONNEL ARGYLLSHIRE

Here an early sunrise can be seen through morning mists rising from the surface of Argyll's Loch Etive; the mountain in the distance is Ben Cruachan. From the slopes of Ben Cruachan, climbers can look down upon the site of the original Clan Campbell's land in Argyllshire. *Cruachan* (pronounced 'crooahan') is the clan's battle cry.

The Campbells have played a prominent part in Scottish history. The line started in the twelfth century, fathered by Sir Colin Campbell of Lochow, also known as Great Colin. There are many famous Campbells and among them was one Mary Campbell of Dunoon, made famous by the love of Robbie Burns. It was Mary who inspired such love poems as 'Highland Mary' and 'The Highland Lassie'. Sadly she died at a young age and Burns, broken-hearted, wrote the beautiful 'To Mary in Heaven' in memory of her.

On a plateau of Ben Cruachan is a natural reservoir of water, fed by the rain and the overflow from nearby Loch Awe. This reservoir has become a vital part of life to people in the surrounding areas, it creates power for the Cruachan Power Station (a hydro-electric power plant) which gives local communities their electricity supply.

Ben Vair Reflected in Glencoe Lochan
GLENCOE ARGYLLSHIRE

In this scene the lochan is as still as glass, reflecting a mirror-like image of the hills around Glencoe. The most prominent of these is the mountain Ben Vair.

There are many legends associated with Glencoe, tales of kelpies rising from the lochs, of spirits inhabiting the mountains and fairies playing in the glen. After the 1692 massacre of the MacDonalds by the Campbells, it is said that fairies appeared to the killers. Under whatever guise they employed, the fairies lured the Campbells away from the path they were following on their return to Fort William. Instead they took them into the mountains and left them to wander for miles off their course.

Synonymous with Glencoe is a simple playing card, the Nine of Diamonds. According to legend, the order for the Campbells to attack was written on that particular card. The order was given by the Master of the Stair, whose heraldic arms bears nine pips, as does the playing card. The Nine of Diamonds has become known as the 'Curse of Scotland', its presence is said to herald doom. Glencoe has become known as the 'Glen of Weeping'.

Red Deer
OBAN ARGYLLSHIRE

Deer are the largest mammal indigenous to Scotland, there are two types that roam the country: the red deer and the roe deer. The red deer are more prolific than the slightly smaller roe deer and their native habitat is the Highlands, where they can usually be seen in abundance. One of the staple foods of the red deer's diet is heather, preferably the young, tender, deliciously juicy shoots of the plant, but autumnal seed capsules will do in lieu of a spring-time feast and the tougher, gristlier winter heather plants are vital to red deer if they are to survive the rigours of a Highland snow.

This photograph captures a quintessential image of Scotland, one which forms the first mental picture in the mind of anyone who has visited the Highlands.

My heart's in the Highlands,
My heart is not here;
My heart's in the Highlands
A-chasing the deer;
Chasing the wild deer,
And following the roe,
My heart's in the Highlands,
Wherever I go.

Robert Burns

Highland Cow
HIGHLAND REGION

The distinctive figure of the Highland Cow has been seen in the Highlands of Scotland for hundreds of years. No sources relate exactly how they first came to the shores, but they are not known to be indigenous. There are written accounts of Highland Cattle dating as far back as the thirteenth century, although the beasts of that time were smaller and, if possible, had even more hair. They were, however the ancestors of the Highland Cattle seen throughout Scotland, and occasionally elsewhere, today.

Few animals can survive the extremes of a Scots winter in the way that a Highland cow is able to. The long, thick, shaggy red coat is invaluable in temperatures of severe cold. In winter, when grass is covered and stifled by thick carpets of snow, the Highland cow relies on heather to add to the food supply provided by farmers. As well as commercially produced cattle foods, farmers in the Highlands provide their cattle with hay and turnips to help them through the cold winter months.

On The slopes of Ben Cruachan
CONNEL ARGYLLSHIRE

From the slopes of Ben Cruachan, sheep farmer Allan Gray and his dog keep an eye on their flocks. The sight is one common in the mountains and pastures of Scotland today, although it was not until the eighteenth and nineteenth centuries that sheep farming became popular in Scotland.

A crisis happened in the clans' society when their landlords began to demand rent from their tenants in cash. Until this time, payment had been by work performed for, often by fighting on behalf of, the laird. As the structure of Scots society changed, particularly in regard to the suppression of clans after the Jacobite rebellions, the lairds began to look elsewhere, finding non-rent paying tenants an expensive encumbrance. It was at this time that the sheep-farming industry began to take hold. Lairds could see that the land would be more lucratively used as sheep-grazing, thereby providing a rich income from the wool, milk and meat provided. Tenants were turned out of their homes, provided with shoddy alternatives or no alternative at all. At that time tenants had no legal status, so the lairds were free to do as they pleased. This type of inhumane eviction became a widespread problem, and has become known as the 'Clearances'.

Cairngorm Mountains
NEAR KINGUSSIE HIGHLAND REGION

The Cairngorms are a massive huddle of mountains, with peaks reaching over 4000ft in height, although geologists claim that, in the mists of the past, the Cairngorms were actually as high as the Himalayas. The range spans the land from Aviemore to Braemar, thereby linking the Rivers Spey and Dee. This view is taken from a site near Kingussie.

These mountains provide Scotland with its most spectacular ski resort, where skiers can look down from the slopes on to one hundred square miles of nature reserve. The mountains and their valleys are home to many species of bird, including mountain eagles, animals and unusual plant forms.

The ruins visible in this photograph are of Ruthven Barracks, built in 1718 and later to be extended by that master of engineering, General Wade. The barracks were built as a base from which the Hanoverian troops could control the Highlanders, but they fell into the hands of the Jacobites, becoming the starting point for the Forty-Five. After the Highlanders' decimating defeat at Culloden, they regrouped, again at Ruthven. Bonnie Prince Charlie was defeated in number and in spirit and could bear no further fighting. His Jacobite supporters destroyed the barracks after realising that their cause was lost.

Ben Nevis
The Nevis Range and Rannoch Moor
PERTHSHIRE

This image of Ben Nevis in the spring shows the Nevis range and the distant Rannoch Moor taken from Banavie, Lochaber. Ben Nevis is perhaps the most spectacular feature of Scotland's northern highlands; it is also the highest mountain in the British Isles and probably the best known. The mountain is 4406ft high. The views from the summit of Ben Nevis are understandably impressive – on a favourable day, it is even possible to see the coast of Ireland. In the early nineteenth century, an observatory was built at the mountain's head, though sadly this was closed in 1904 and now all that remains of the building is ruins.

The land around Rannoch is also a place of splendour. As well as the rolling, purple moor, the area is home to the Black Wood of Rannoch, a shelter of wonderfully ancient trees. Many of the trees date back to the time of the grand, all encompassing Caledonian Forest – a forest which covered almost all of Scotland in former, less-populated, centuries. It spread from Glen Lyon to Rannoch Moor and from Glencoe to the Braes of Mar. The forest was destroyed and burned by the rulers of the country in an effort to stamp out the danger imposed by outlaws, highwaymen, wolves and bears who inhabited the mass of trees.

View to the Cairngorms from Loch Morlich
HIGHLAND REGION

The Cairngorms are the highest mountain range in the British Isles; they extend for 2000 square miles and encompass peaks of over 4000ft. They are also home to a wonderful array of plant and bird life. These include ptarmigans, a species of bird that has been around in the Cairngorms since the Ice Age; dotterels, a type of bird whose male tends the eggs and chicks while the female finds another male to mate with and the rare snow bunting. On one of the mountains is a sub-Arctic plateau, home to animals and plants seen nowhere else in this part of the world.

There are also semi-permanent snow fields containing remnants of the long-gone Caledonian Forest and showing ravages in the granite slopes that were caused by the last Ice Age. In 1935, an area of the forest was chosen and renamed in honour of the Silver Jubilee of King George V and Queen Mary. The name given to the area was Queen's Forest.

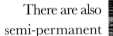

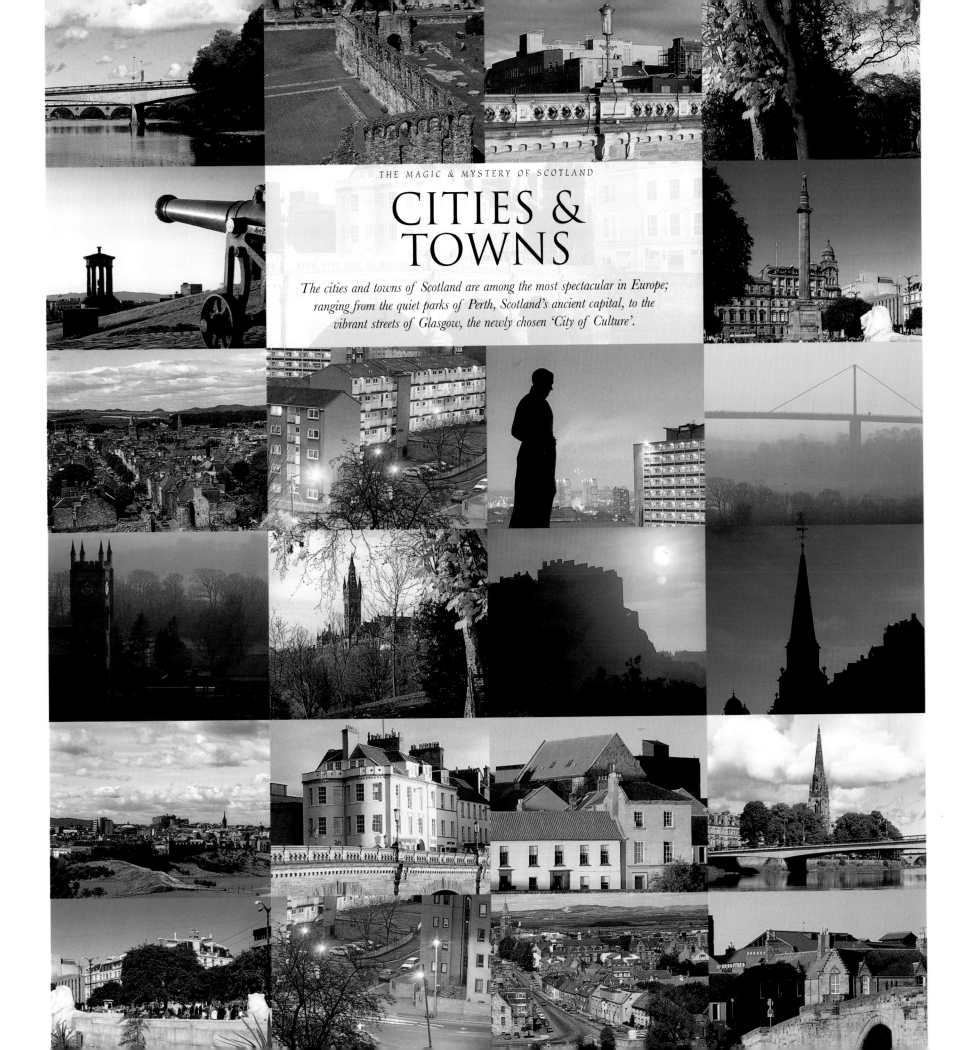

CITIES &
TOWNS

The cities and towns of Scotland are among the most spectacular in Europe;
ranging from the quiet parks of Perth, Scotland's ancient capital, to the
vibrant streets of Glasgow, the newly chosen 'City of Culture'.

Cathedral and Town
ST ANDREWS FIFE PENINSULA

This view of St Andrews cathedral and town can be seen from St Rules Tower. The tower is named after the saint who brought the bones of St Andrew to Scotland in the fourth century. St Andrew became the patron saint of Scotland.

According to unsubstantiated legend, St Andrew's remains were taken from Greece, the place of his martyrdom, by St Rule (also called St Regulus). The boat in which St Rule was travelling was shipwrecked and both saints – the one alive, the other dead – were washed up on the shore of Scotland, at the place now called St Andrews. By the eighth century, a settlement had grown up around the present city's site, and a chapel had been established on the shore.

St Andrew is said to provide help when his people need it. In the tenth century a great and deadly battle took place between the Picts and the Northumbrians. The Picts defeated their enemy and, after the victory, it is said that they looked up to the heavens. There they beheld the diagonal white cross of St Andrew defined against a clear blue sky.

View from the Necropolis
GLASGOW

This dramatic, early nightime view of Glasgow was taken from the Necropolis, graveyard of the merchants, close to St Mungo's cathedral.

The first saint to bless the site on which Glasgow's cathedral now stands was St Ninian, in the fifth century. However, it was the sixth-century St Mungo who built the first church on the site, and it is from him that the present cathedral takes its name. St Mungo is also the patron saint of Glasgow.

During his lifetime, St Mungo performed several miracles for his people and three of these are recorded in the city's coat of arms. Glasgow's crest includes the symbols of a tree, a salmon with a ring in its mouth and a bird. The tree recalls the time when the monastery fire went out in the dead of winter; St Mungo had enough faith to relight the fire with just a frozen branch. The salmon is symbolic of the time St Mungo helped a queen in distress, by finding the ring, given to her by the king, which she had lost; he saw it in the belly of a salmon and returned it to her. The bird denotes the time the saint revived a robin after its head had been cut off.

Old Kilpatrick Church and Erskine Bridge
GLASGOW

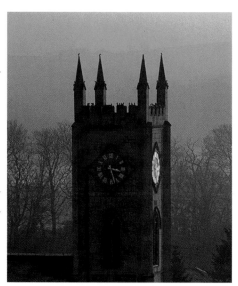

This atmospheric evening view of the Erskine Bridge also shows a misty view of Old Kilpatrick Church, its tower clock glinting in the light of the setting sun. Erskine Bridge is a toll bridge and one of Glasgow's main thoroughfares, leading traffic over the River Clyde and into the heart of the city.

The River Clyde was the reason for Glasgow's wealth and success in the eighteenth and nineteenth centuries. In the eighteenth century, the Forth Clyde canal was built, linking the two major cities of Edinburgh and Glasgow and, therefore, both sides of the country. During the Industrial Revolution of the nineteenth century, Glasgow became a place of prosperity and fashion, because of its prominent position on such a major water course. All along the Clyde sprung up shipyards and factories. Industry was booming and merchants were suddenly abundant, trading throughout the world and bringing wealth to the city.

On the site at which Old Kilpatrick Church now stands has been found the remains of a Roman fort, looking back to the time when the Roman Empire still entertained hopes of taming and controlling the land of the Picts.

View from Kelvingrove Park
GLASGOW

Glasgow University is seen here from Kelvingrove Park on an auburn autumn afternoon. The history of Glasgow's university dates back to 1451 when it was founded by a Bishop. Bishop Turnbull's first classes were held in the crypt of St Mungo's cathedral, before a building could be found.

Glasgow University houses the Hunterian Art Gallery, home to several paintings by Whistler as well as a celebration of the life and works of the celebrated Glaswegian artist, Charles Rennie Mackintosh. Mackintosh's renowned architecture can be seen in many districts of Glasgow, perhaps most notably in his Glasgow School of Art.

Kelvingrove Park flanks the River Kelvin, a small tributary of the city's main waterway, the River Clyde. The design for the park was laid out in 1852 by an eminent landscape architect, Joseph Paxton, and was named for Lord William Thompson Kelvin, a prominent phsyicist and professor of the University of Glasgow. Kelvin was born in 1824 and died in 1907, fifty-three of those years were dedicated to the university. A monument to him can be found in the park, along with monuments to the writer Thomas Carlyle and the medical pioneer Joseph Lister.

Edinburgh Castle and St Cuthbert's
EDINBURGH

The dramatic silhouette of Edinburgh's castle and St Cuthbert's church, can be seen from West Princes Street Gardens. As the sun sets behind the castle rock, the dominance the castle has over the rest of the city is profound.

The city of Edinburgh is divided into two parts: the Old Town and the New Town. The Old Town has been a settlement for centuries and the rock, on which Edinburgh Castle now stands, bears Bronze Age remains dating back to *c.* 1000 BC. Since that time, there appears to have been a fortress of some kind on the castle rock. The earliest part of the present castle dates back to the seventh century, when Edwin of Northumbria, from whom Edinburgh takes its name, conquered the city and built his defence base on the rock. The castle has been added to continuously since Edwin's time and the stones used to build it could tell a thousand tales of the city's turbulent history.

Edinburgh Castle stands at the stately head of the city's main thoroughfare, the Royal Mile. It is so called because it is the road which links the castle, at the head of the mile, with the Palace of Holyroodhouse at the mile's foot.

Salisbury Crags
EDINBURGH

Salisbury Crags are sited south-east of Edinburgh, beyond St Margaret's and Dunsapie Lochs. This photograph, taken on a clear-skied day shows the rugged magnificence of the hills in fine contrast to the carefully landscaped city; the the panoramic view emphasising their height and enormity. Beneath the blue of a summer sky, Edinburgh's skyline appears in crisp detail, a skyline which is dominated by the magnificent castle and the imposing, gothic Scott Memorial. Edinburgh is a city of perfectly blended history and modernity, its fascinating culture and eminently Scots atmosphere mingle harmoniously. As can be seen, the wilder side of Scotland is never far away, even in the capital city.

Near the foot of the crags is the village of Duddingston, remembered in history as the place where the Young Pretender's army camped in 1745. At Duddingston there is a church which dates back to Norman times. Curiously, the church has a watchtower – not to guard against invaders as may be supposed, but to keep watch for bodysnatchers raiding the cemetery!

Bridge in Ayr town centre
AYRSHIRE

The stunning evening light warms the stones of Ayr town centre and its perfectly reflected bridge. Ayr has an impressive history: it is known to have been a settlement as far back as the eighth century AD and, throughout time, has been associated with names such as William Wallace; King William I, the Lion (who gave the town its first charter in 1202); Robert the Bruce; King James IV; Oliver Cromwell and Scotland's favourite son, Robert Burns.

In 1297 Ayr was the site of William Wallace's attack on England, when his army burnt the 'barns of Ayr' in which the English soldiers were encamped and, in 1298, the castle which used to guard the town of Ayr, was destroyed by Robert the Bruce to prevent its occupation by the English. From 1314, Bruce was hailed as Scotland's rightful king, and it was in Ayr, in the old church of St John, that the parliament met to discuss the succession of the Scottish crown in the event of his death.

Evening Light over Berwick-upon-Tweed
THE BORDERS

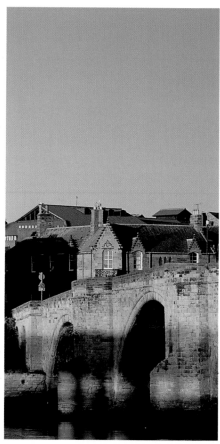

Berwick-upon-Tweed has had a confused history. The town whose name is known throughout the world for its famous material, has been bandied between Scotland and England for hundreds of years. Officially the property of England, Berwick's history is the history of Scotland's people.

It was King David I (1124–53) who first claimed Berwick for the Scots. He extended his country's border southwards, recognising Berwick as a logistically important vantage point from which to keep an eye on the English. Over the years that ensued, the town was used as a pawn in the battle between the two countries, constantly being lost and won by both sides.

The English recovered Berwick-upon-Tweed in 1482, under Richard, Duke of Gloucester, later King Richard III. The town was won during the Duke's campaign to occupy Edinburgh, which he did for a while, under the orders of a contrary King Edward IV. The king had agreed a truce between England and Scotland, settled by the betrothal of his daughter Cecilia to the prince of Scotland, but broke his pact when he transferred his affections, and the hand of his daughter, to the French court. Hostilities between England and Scotland were resumed as a result. Since that day, Berwick-upon-Tweed has been a part of England.

City of Perth
TAYSIDE PERTHSHIRE

Perth is a city with a long history. The straight planning of its roads suggests that it was originally settled by the Romans, although there is no concrete evidence to support this. What is certain is that Perth, as founded by King William the Lion in 1210, was Scotland's capital city until the mid-fifteenth century.

In 1266, the Scots signed a contract with Norway, who had long been battling to gain control of the country. In the Treaty of Perth, the Norwegians conceded all their possessions to Scotland except for the Orkneys and Shetlands. In return, Scotland was to pay an annual fee to Norway as well as a lump sum when the treaty was signed.

This view of the city of Perth can be seen from the shore of the River Tay, along whose west side the city is located. In 1396, the river's north bank witnessed a lethal clash of the clans: Clan Chattan and Clan Quhele fought one another, with thirty men on each side, most of whom were killed. The victors, were Clan Chattan, though their number was severely depleted and many of their best warriors were killed. The battle provided inspiration for Sir Walter Scott who used it in his novel *The Maid of Perth*.

Calton Hill
EDINBURGH

Calton Hill, in North-East Edinburgh, is one of two major vantage points from which to view the city. The other is Arthur's seat. This photograph of the hill's summit shows a memorial cannon and a monument to Robert Burns. Calton Hill also bears a monument to Nelson, and a half-finished memorial to those Scots who fell in the Napoleonic Wars. Plans for a large, Grecian style temple were submitted in 1822, but sadly the costly process was abandoned when lack of funds made it impossible and today what looks like a noble ancient ruin is all that remains of a once-lofty ideal.

Arthur's Seat rises from Holyrood Park to a height of 822ft. The Arthur to whom it refers may be forever shrouded in mystery: some say it is named after the legendary King Arthur of Camelot, but no evidence has been found; alternatively if may refer to a sixth-century Prince Arthur of Strathclyde, again unsubstantiated. Other sources suggest the name comes from the less romantic story of a criminal named Arthur who was bound and perished at the hill's summit and yet another surmise is that the name comes from the lengthy Gaelic *ard-na-saighaid* meaning 'height of the flight of arrows'. Each theory is, without concrete evidence, as likely as the next.

George Square
GLASGOW

George Square is the heart of Glasgow. Its design was laid out in 1781 and its name derives from King George III. The King was intended to be immortalised here in the form of a statue – but it was the novelist Sir Walter Scott who achieved that honour.

It is Scott's statue that dominates the square through its massive height. The figure of the writer, sculpted by John Greenshields, stands at the top of an eighty foot doric column created by David Rhind. The memorial was completed in 1837 and has gained fame by being the first Scots monument ever to be dedicated to a literary figure. The stone lions seen in this picture flank the city's cenotaph, built after the First World War by John Burbett, to honour Scotland's dead.

Other statues in the square include those of Robert Burns, Sir John Moore (a Glaswegian war hero), prime ministers Gladstone and Peel, the engineer James Watt and the royal couple Queen Victoria and Prince Albert. Sir John Moore's was the first statue to be placed in the square, in 1819, but it is Scott's that remains the most impressive. Ironically, the most prominent statue in Glasgow is of a citizen of Edinburgh.

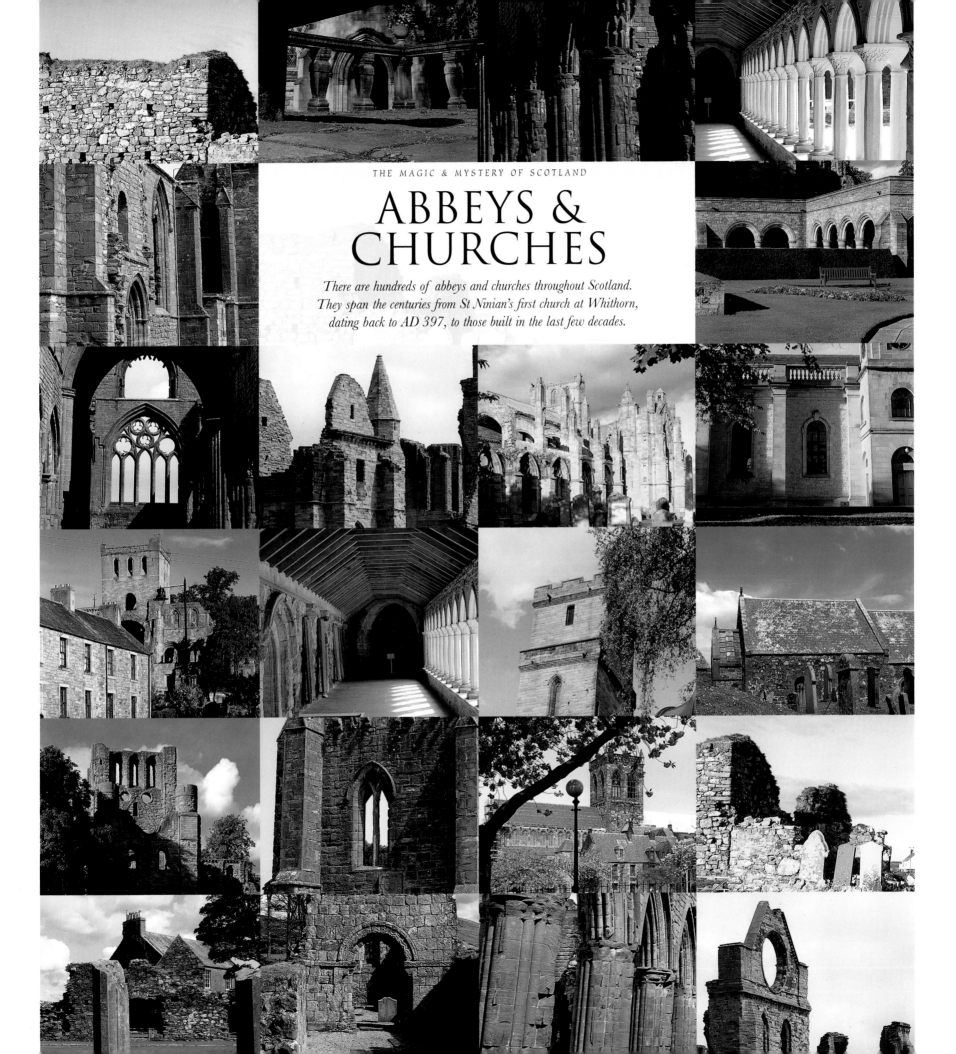

ABBEYS & CHURCHES

There are hundreds of abbeys and churches throughout Scotland. They span the centuries from St Ninian's first church at Whithorn, dating back to AD 397, to those built in the last few decades.

Sweetheart Abbey
NEW ABBEY VILLAGE DUMFRIESSHIRE

The story of how the ruined Sweetheart Abbey came by its name, is a truly romantic legend. The abbey dates back to 1273, when it was founded by a woman named Devorguilla Balliol, in memory of her husband. This remarkable woman also gave her name Balliol college at Oxford University, the college she founded.

Devorguilla survived her husband by seventeen years, living until the age of ninety – an almost unheard of age for the thirteenth century. Throughout the seventeen years of widowhood, she carried her husband's heart with her, no matter where she went. After her death in 1290, Devorguilla, together with the heart of her husband, was buried in front of the high altar in Sweetheart Abbey, known at the time by its Latin name of *Dulce Cor.*

The fate of the abbey was unfortunately sealed during the Reformation. Sweetheart's abbot, Gilbert Brown, was vociferous in his condemnation of the movement and therefore the last to preside over this once-glorious building. Today the tomb of the devoted Balliols lies in the reconstructed south transept. As can be seen from this beautifully evocative photograph, the abbey is splendid even in ruins.

Arbroath Abbey
ANGUS

The graceful ruins of this red sandstone abbey date back to 1178, and the murder of Thomas à Becket. Thomas was a prominent figure in the English court of King Henry II (1133–1189), appointed Chancellor to the King and later created Archbishop of Canterbury. Their friendship flourished until Becket refused to accede to Henry's dream of a Church and State alliance. Henry's now famous and ill-fated cry, 'Who will rid me of this turbulent priest?', was heard by four over-zealous knights of his court. Eager to gain favour, they rode to Canterbury Cathedral on the night of 29 December 1170, and there they slew the Archbishop on hallowed ground – the steps of the altar. Henry was appalled and, when Becket was canonised just three years later, led a barefoot pilgrimage to his shrine.

The murder led to a furious rebellion led by Scotland's King William the Lion (1165–1214), in the company of many English landowners. In 1174 William was defeated and captured, on the same day, as he later discovered, that Henry II underwent penance by scourging. The religious import of this coincidence impressed William deeply. On his release from captivity, he founded Arbroath Abbey and dedicated it to the memory of St Becket.

Melrose Abbey
MELROSE THE BORDERS

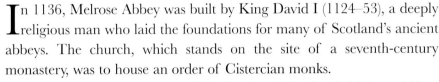

In 1136, Melrose Abbey was built by King David I (1124–53), a deeply religious man who laid the foundations for many of Scotland's ancient abbeys. The church, which stands on the site of a seventh-century monastery, was to house an order of Cistercian monks.

Located on the border of England and Scotland, Melrose Abbey was unfortunately in the line of fire at many a battle between the countries. In 1322, the English destroyed King David's abbey, but the building was restored by Robert the Bruce in 1326. Bruce bequeathed his heart to the abbey and, when he died in 1329, it was reputedly brought here for internment; the rest of his body is buried at Dunfermline.

The English demolished the abbey again in 1385, after which it was rebuilt a second time. Most of the present building dates back to this time, although further work was carried out in the mid-fifteenth and seventeenth centuries. This stunning view seen in the early evening light, shows the spectacular, slightly eerie aspect of the abbey, claimed by many to be the most beautiful in Scotland. The abbey also houses the tomb of Scotland's famous 'flying wizard', Michael Scot. The opening of Scot's grave is mentioned in Sir Walter Scott's *The Lay of the Last Minstrel*.

Melrose Church
MELROSE THE BORDERS

Throughout history, the Borders town of Melrose has suffered much in-fighting between the Scots and English. One such incident took place in 1385, when King Richard II heard that French troops had arrived on the shores, in a bid to ally themselves with Scotland against England. As part of the King's campaign of punishment, his soldiers set fire to the towns of Melrose, Edinburgh, Dundee and Perth.

The original Parish Church of Melrose was built between 1808 and 1810, by the architect John Smith. Unfortunately, it was destroyed by a virulent fire less than a hundred years after completion, leaving only the church tower still standing. In 1911, the architect J. M. Peddie fought off fierce competition and won the contract to re-build the church. His Georgian revivalist design, and the use of the original stone, were fittingly complementary to the bereft tower; as can be seen here, in the gentle glow of an autumn afternoon. The church is situated at the top of Weir Hill, from where beautiful views of the surrounding countryside can found.

Jedburgh Abbey
JEDBURGH THE BORDERS

This unusual view of Jedburgh Abbey was taken from the Jed Water on a crisp autumnal day. The abbey was built between the twelfth and fifteenth centuries, on a site that had been revered by Christians for several hundred years. It is known that in the ninth century a chapel was standing in Jedburgh, this became a priory founded by David I (1124–53) in *c.*1138. From his foundations, the abbey was born.

As with all buildings sited at The Borders, Jedburgh Abbey found itself in the line of fire during Scots and English hostilities. The most disastrous moment in its history was the abject destruction caused by the Earl of Hertford in 1545. Hertford was the brother of Jane Seymour, Henry VIII's third wife, who managed to avoid losing her head, by dying while giving birth to Henry's longed-for son. It was this son, Edward, who was to cause the Scots so much grief. When Henry's intended match, between Edward and the infant Mary, was rejected by Scotland, Hertford and his army were sent as punishment; a mission Hertford appeared to carry out with zealous bloodlust. After the Reformation, a part of the ruined abbey was salvaged to become Jedburgh's parish church.

Monastic Cloisters
IONA, INNER HEBRIDES

Iona of my heart, Iona of my love
Instead of monks' voices there shall be
lowing of cattle:
But before the world comes to an end
Iona shall be as it was.
The Last Words of St Columba

There is a legend that claims that when the rest of the world has been covered by the sea, the stalwart island of Iona will remain alone. Iona is the earliest centre of Christianity in Scotland and, as such, it was the religious epicentre for the entire Celtic world. This photograph shows the restored cloisters that join the medieval monastic buildings to their Abbey.

Not far from Iona Abbey stands an eleventh-century chapel, dedicated to St Oran. This humble church is also the last resting place of Kings; here the bones of Duncan I (1034–40) and Macbeth (1040–57) lie entwined with the bones of forty-six other Kings of Scotland, as well as the skeletal remains of Kings from Ireland, France and Norway. In centuries past, the last journey of a king from these foreign lands would be by boat to this small Scottish island. Only then could he be laid to rest.

Church of the Holyrood
STIRLING STIRLING REGION

'Holyrood', sometimes written as 'Holy Rude', comes from the Gaelic and means 'holy cross'. It was in this church that the young Mary of Guise was crowned Queen of Scots in 1544; this was also the place of her one-year-old grandson's coronation, as King James VI – the small child who was later to become James I of England and one of political history's most influential figures.

Stirling's original inhabitants are something of a mystery; the name is possibly from Welsh, meaning 'place of striving', so Stirling's founders may well have arrived from Wales. Other possible conquerors include the Romans, the Saxons and the legendary King Arthur; however all these possible inhabitants are unverified. The first proven king to have been associated with Stirling was Alexander I, who died in the castle in 1124; it is also known to have been one of the favourite places of King Alexander III, who reigned from 1249 to 1286.

The cannon seen at the front of the picture, set into a concrete block, is one of several captured at the Battle of Sevastopol during the Crimean War; it is embossed with the Russian eagle. The captors were soldiers of the Argyll and Southern Highlanders, whose current head-quarters is Stirling Castle.

Kirkmadrine Chapel
KIRKMADRINE RHINNS OF GALLOWAY

The churchyard of Kirkmadrine Chapel is home to the Kirkmadrine Stones, some of the oldest Christian relics in Britain. The introduction of Christianity into Scotland took place around 400 BC, with the landing of St Ninian at Whithorn, not far from here. The Kirkmadrine Stones seem to date from just a few years after the saint's arrival. St Ninian was a local man who had journeyed to Rome to study; when he returned to his homeland he constructed Scotland's first church, made from Galloway stone.

The decorated cross at the left-hand side of the picture is a fine example of early Christian Celtic art, though it is not as old as the Kirkmadrine Stones. The stones themselves also bear decorations, some of them Latin inscriptions together with the 'chi-rho' symbol a secret Christian emblem formed in times of persecution to enable Christians to identify one another. The symbol is formed from the first two Greek letters of Christ's name.

The Rhinns of Galloway is a double peninsula jutting out from Scotland's south-west corner, with the beautiful Mull of Galloway forming the southernmost tip. When seen from the air, the stretch of land is shaped like a hammer's head.

Ruins of Kelso Abbey from the Gardens

KELSO THE BORDERS

Kelso's illustrious abbey, now just a haunting ruin, dates back to 1128. It was built by an order of French monks from Picardy; they constructed their place of worship on foundations laid by King David I (1124–53), the abbey's founder.

According to a description from 1517, the Abbey had the unusual aspect of two transepts; this apparently followed an ambitious ground plan reflecting the shape of the cross of Lorraine. The small portion of the building that remains today, belies its original, considerable, size: the stones left standing are most likely the remains of just one wing of the monastery. Kelso Abbey was probably the largest of all the border abbeys, a reflection of its importance and that of the monks' order. At one time the abbot of Kelso was held in higher ecumenical regard than even the abbot of St Andrews, but it was a short-lived exultation. Kelso's position on the border of Scotland and England made its safety precarious and it was often the scene of attack. In 1545 the abbey was razed to the ground and all inhabitants, including 12 monks, were slaughtered.

Fortrose Cathedral
BLACK ISLE ROSS AND CROMARTY INVERNESS-SHIRE

Fortrose and Cromarty are the two main towns of the Black Isle – a picturesque, though strangely named, area of Scotland, which is a peninsula of the mainland, not an island. The ruined and roofless Fortrose Cathedral is in the centre of Fortrose town, an impressive red sandstone remain, which harks back to the time of King David I (1124–53), that tireless builder of abbeys, and has stood staunchly, through glory and ruination for over eight hundred years.

A church on the foundations built by King David was used as a fortress by the supporters of two of Scotland's greatest defenders, William Wallace and Robert the Bruce. It also played a vital role in the army's morale as the troops believed that, with the Cathedral as their headquarters, they had God on their side.

The existing building was extended in the fifteenth century by the Abbot of Melrose, soon to become Abbot Fraser of Fortrose. In the seventeenth century, Oliver Cromwell's troops wreaked havoc on the sacred building when robbing stone; they needed it to build Cromwell a fortress at Inverness. Since then, Fortrose Cathedral has remained almost as they left it, just a nave and a bell tower echoing the past.

Paisley Abbey
PAISLEY RENFREWSHIRE

The original Paisley Abbey was a large imposing building; though only a small part of it remains today. This colourful photograph, seen from the perfect vantage point of a glorious spring day, shows the abbey as it stands now; just the nave of the earlier, much larger church.

The first Christian building on this site was founded by Walter Fitzalan, an ancestor of Robert the Bruce. He came to Paisley from Shropshire, promising to house thirteen monks of the Cluniac order in a priory he would build for them. The site he chose had previously been home to the cell of St Mirren, a martyr of the seventh century. The saint's relics were transferred to the new priory and the monks' new building quickly became a place of pilgrimage.

In the nineteenth century, Renfrewshire was the cotton capital of Scotland, producing materials, threads and rope; the area also produced the world-famous Paisley Pattern and led some of Scotland's most lucrative industries, such as engineering and shipbuilding. Paisley became most famed for its production of Paisley shawls, a Scottish interpretation of the highly fashionable nineteenth-century Indian shawls.

Teampull na Trioaids Monastery
CARINISH, NORTH UIST OUTER HEBRIDES

Teampull na Trioiads means 'Trinity Temple'. These unusual ruins, sited on the picturesque island of North Uist, are on the site of a previous Celtic settlement. It is thought that Beatrix, daughter of the warrior Somerled, father of the MacDonald clan, built the first Christian structure here. The church, which was made up of two buildings, was later repaired by the daughter of King Robert II (1371–1390), wife of the First Lord of the Isles. It is the ruins of her building that can be seen today. Many centuries ago, *Teampull na Trioiads* was a renowned centre of great spiritual learning.

North Uist is home to many wonderful monuments and relics from ages past. At the top of Blashaval hill are three standing stones; these are known as *Na Fir Bhreige* ('three false men'). According to legend, the standing stones mark the graves of three spies – who were buried alive. There is also a chambered cairn, dating back to Neolithic times, and edifices which remain from the Iron Age.

Ruins of Luce Abbey
GLENLUCE GALLOWAY

Luce Abbey was the home of Michael Scot, the wizard of Scotland. Scot was an incredible figure: an alchemist, scholar, astrologer, cleric, mathematician, linguist, occultist and believed magician. He studied at the court of Frederick II in Rome where he worked as a translator, changing texts from Arabic and Greek into Latin. Later he returned to Scotland and is attributed to having tamed the plague: luring it to Luce Abbey and imprisoning it within a deep vault. Scot was believed to have discovered the secret of flying and apparently flew to Rome to visit the Pope. He is also said to have possessed a demon horse and ship to assist him in his occult dealings and apparently foretold his own death. Exactly when he died is unknown and the dates for his life range from 1117 to 1235 – perhaps he also knew a spell for longevity.

The abbey dates back to 1192, when it was founded by Roland, Earl of Galloway. It was commissioned as a daughter abbey to Dundrennan, which was built fifty years previously. Dundrennan is best known for its place in history on the night of 15 May 1568: it was the last place that Mary, Queen of Scots, rested in before leaving Scotland for England.

Sᴛ Blane's Chapel
GARROCH HEAD BUTE ARGYLLSHIRE

St Blane was a sixth-century Scot, who studied in Ireland and returned home to preach Christianity and found a monastery on the Isle of Bute. These twelfth-century ruins were named after him and are on his monastery's site. He chose a picturesque, peaceful part of the island, called Garroch Head, from where one can look across the sea to the Isle of Arran. An interesting fact about the later chapel is that it had two cemeteries: one for men and one for women. It is said that if a man was ever buried in the women's cemetery, or a woman ever buried in the men's; the bodies would disinter themselves overnight.

Bute is also home to the fourteenth-century St Mary's Chapel, sited just outside the capital, Rothesay. Although not as historically renowned as St Blane's Chapel, St Mary's houses a famous tomb – that of Stephanie Hortense Bonaparte, a niece of Napoleon.

The island of Bute is fifteen miles long and five miles wide, with two distinct geographical areas; these are created by the Highland Boundary Fault, out of which grew the impressive Loch Fad. During the Victorian era, Bute was a very popular tourist area. It was easy to reach from Glasgow and the island's capital, Rothesay, became highly fashionable.

THE MAGIC & MYSTERY OF SCOTLAND

CASTLES & PALACES

*Throughout history over three hundred castles have stood in Scotland.
Many are now evocative ruins, home only to memories of the past, but
some are still inhabited by the descendants of those who built them.*

Blair Castle
BLAIR ATHOLL PERTHSHIRE

This evening view of Blair Castle, provides a wonderful contrast of colours, with the brilliant white of the building against the muted colours of the surrounding landscape. Although building work on the original castle dates back to the thirteenth century, there have been constant changes and additions and the main bulk of the structure now appears mainly eighteenth and nineteenth century in origin. As it looks today, Blair Castle is a spectacular example of a Scotch Baronial mansion; the style of architecture so firmly espoused by the talented Glaswegian architect Charles Rennie Mackintosh.

The grounds surrounding the castle are perhaps most noteworthy for their magnificent trees. The road leading up to the castle's entrance is flanked by an elegant avenue of lime trees and throughout the parkland surrounding the ancient seat of the Atholls, are trees which could reveal secrets about many of the castle's eminent visitors. King Edward III; Mary, Queen of Scots; Oliver Cromwell and Queen Victoria have all spent time beneath the pointed roofs of this castle. Robert Burns also visited and wrote a poem entitled 'The Humble Petition of Bruar Water'. The poem was actually a criticism of the lack of trees around the castle's natural waterfall. As a result the waterfall now resides in a thickly wooded haven.

Castle Stalker
NEAR APPIN ARGYLLSHIRE

A lowering sky only adds to the magnificence of Castle Stalker, in Argyllshire. The castle takes its name from the Gaelic 'Caisteal Stalcair', its literal translation is 'castle of the hunter'. This sixteenth-century edifice, built by the Stewarts of Appin as a family home, resides majestically on its own islet not far from the town of Appin. The view from the castle includes the picturesque Isle of Lismore, famed for its strong religious community dating back through the centuries and its Celtic connections.

The town of Appin is probably best known through Robert Louis Stevenson's novels *Kidnapped* and *Catriona*, as the place of the infamous Appin murder of 1742. When Colin Campbell, also known as the 'Red Fox', was shot in 1752, his wound proved fatal. The murderer escaped and was never found, but the Clan Campbell were baying for justice and blood. Cruelly thirsting for revenge, a Campbell judge and jury sentenced the innocent 'James of the Glens', a member of the Clan Stewart, to death by hanging. The appointed executioner was also a Campbell.

Barcaldine Castle in Winter
LOCH CRERAN ARGYLLSHIRE

Argyll's Barcaldine Castle dates from the early seventeenth century when it was built by Black Duncan of the Cowl, who lived from 1546 to 1631. Black Duncan was the seventh knight and first baronet of Glenorchy, and ancestor of the Breadalbane line of the Clan Campbell. In fact it was one of Black Duncan's descendants who was notoriously murdered – and avenged – at Appin in 1752.

Black Duncan built Barcaldine Castle, one of seven that he built during his lifetime, in 1609. He gave it to his son, Patrick. The castle stands on the south shore of Loch Creran, not far from the town of Oban. Throughout its history, the castle has spent most of its life owned by members of the Campbell family, although it was sold to an outsider in the mid-nineteenth century. From 1842 onwards, the castle remained outside Campbell ownership for half a century, until Sir Duncan Campbell, the third baronet of Barcaldine, bought back his ancestral home in 1896. From that day on, Barcaldine Castle has remained in the hands of Black Duncan's descendants.

View from Fort George Battlements
NAIRNSHIRE

Fort George was the the brainchild of the English King George II, who reigned between 1727 and 1760. After the Jacobite rebellion of 1745–46, the Hanoverian monarchy felt threatened and determined never to allow the Scots hordes to threaten them again. Fort George was declared the answer – it would be the ultimate in defence.

The fort took twenty-one years to build, starting in 1748, and cost George II's administration £200,000. Its defences cover forty-two acres of land, with the walls alone running for almost a mile. The designer of the construction was Robert Adam, one of Scotland's most talented architects of the time. An earlier Fort George had been built in Inverness by General Wade, but had been destroyed by one of Bonnie Prince Charlie's French engineers. The engineer was also killed in the blast, but his dog survived, losing only its tail!

The view in this photograph shows the sight from the battlements, protected by a sturdy cannon; from this picture, one can realise the potential of the fort's defence, visually following the cannon shot to its destination. The cannon seen here has never needed to be used in anger – despite King George's fears, Fort George has not experienced a single battle.

Dirleton Castle
DIRLETON EAST LOTHIAN

There has been a protective stronghold guarding the East Lothian town of Dirleton since the twelfth century, but the original structure was made of wood. Today, Dirleton Castle is a still-defiant ruin of a thirteenth-century edifice and, were it not for the barbarism of the English Cromwellian army, the castle might never have fallen into ruins at all.

A proud structure, the castle had defied battles, sieges and even an honourable surrender without more than superficial damage, but the troops of Oliver Cromwell's regime laid waste to that which four centuries of wars could not diminish.

Within the castle grounds, there can still be found the remains of a seventeenth-century bowling green and a beautifully laid-out garden. There is also a dovecote dating back three hundred years, once home to over a thousand birds. Although the beauty of white doves is often romantically illustrated in art and literature, the birds were kept for unaesthetic reasons – they were a valuable supply of fresh meat in the harshness of a Scottish winter.

Edinburgh Castle and Fountain
FROM PRINCES STREET EDINBURGH

Edinburgh Castle has been the site of historical happenings for over a millenium. It has been beseiged, haunted, conquered and used as a barricade and is now one of Scotland's premier tourist attractions, but despite its twentieth-century surroundings, nothing can detract from the the majesty of its history and the atmosphere held within its walls.

A tour of the castle overwhelms the visitor with an incredible amount of information that continually bombards the senses, and the history that drips from every robust wedge of stone. Within the grounds is a witches' well, notoriously marking the execution site of over three hundred women accused of witchcraft, who were burned alive. The last execution took place in 1722. Deep in the castle's bowels rests the enormous cannon Mons Meg, created in Mons in Belgium in the fifteenth century and used against the English by King James IV in 1497. There

are dungeons that housed prisoners of war in centuries past and seem still to moan with the thirst and pain of foreign soldiers. Yet there are peaceful places in the castle as well, such as the tiny and exquisite twelfth-century chapel of the gentle Queen Margaret or the miniature, tombstone-studded cemetery housing the bodies of the guarding soldiers' beloved dogs.

Claypotts Castle
NEAR DUNDEE ANGUS

Claypotts Castle dates from the sixteenth century. The structure is the most complete example of a tower house left in Scotland today. Its architectural style is known as Z-plan, because of the projecting towers at diagonal corners of the building, this style is distinctive to tower houses of this era.

The building was begun in 1569, by one John Strachan. He built his family's new home on land which his father had leased from the nearby Abbey – at the time the abbot of Lindores was one of the most influential figures in Angus. Claypotts Castle passed down through a straight line of three John Strachans.

At the end of the sixteenth century, a change came to Claypotts. After the Reformation, the Abbot of Lindores had lost his high social standing and the area came under the influence of the Barony of Lindores. As a result, the Strachans sold their family home, after just thirty-two years, and moved north. Claypotts Castle's new owner was Sir William Graham. In turn, the castle passed to his son David, who appears to have been the last owner to have lived in the castle. Today, Claypotts Castle is owned by the Home family and is managed by Historic Scotland.

Kilchurn Castle from Loch Awe
ARGYLLSHIRE

The picturesque ruins of Kilchurn Castle, photographed here in the evocative light of a misty dawn, are sited on the north-east side of Loch Awe, on a spit of land jutting into the water. The earliest known date for the castle is 1440. Kilchurn was built by Sir Colin Campbell and intended as the seat to the Lordship of Glen Orchy, and a home for his son and heir.

In the early seventeenth century, a marauding gang of the clan MacGregor attacked Kilchurn. The warriors were beaten off by Sir Duncan Campbell and, from 1614–19, he repaired the damage. In 1693, the site was added to by the first Earl of Breadalbane (a Campbell descendant) and, above the main portals, were placed the crests and initials of the Earl and his wife. These can still be seen today.

The aristocratic family occupied the castle until the eighteenth-century Jacobite rebellions; Jacobites were supporters of King James (II of England, VII of Scotland), the grandfather of Bonnie Prince Charlie. It was in 1745, the year of the second rebellion ('The Forty Five'), that the Breadalbanes were ousted from their home, by English soldiers and the castle became a Hanoverian garrison. In 1775, Kilchurn's roof caved in and was never re-built. It has remained uninhabited ever since.

Eilean Donan Castle

LOCH DUICH INVERNESS-SHIRE

This early morning scene shows the restored Eilean Donan castle in perfect reflection. The castle, viewed here from the shore of Loch Duich, is sited on an islet at the point where three lochs merge. The castle is linked to Loch Duich's shore by an archway.

Far back in time, the castle's site was home to an Iron Age fort, a building which was turned into a castle under the patronage of King Alexander II (1214–49); he used Eilean Donan as a site from which to repel the Vikings. The castle's history became ever more fanciful after the reign of Alexander. Successful in deterring the raiders from the north, and secure throughout several centuries as a peacetime residence, it was thrown back into the thick of battle after becoming a garrison for Spanish soldiers in 1719. Later that same year, Eilean Donan gained the dubious honour of being the first Scots castle to be blown up by a warship – the galleon was positioned in the nearby waters and manned by the English navy.

For almost 200 years the castle remained a ruin, but, at the beginning of the twentieth century, was restored. Now it is one of is the Highland's top tourist attractions, with displays relating the history of the area and its people.

Dunbeath Castle
CAITHNESS

Dunbeath Castle can be seen here from a Caithness shore. The dramatic foreground view of the rust-coloured pancake rocks contrasts stunningly with the castle's sturdy silhouette atop vivid green cliffs. Both elements provide the viewer with a glimpse of a time gone past, a historic building in tandem with an ancient landscape

This area of Caithness has been home to settlers since before the time of the Picts. An Iron Age settlement, or 'broch', has been uncovered near the site of the present castle and written records of local history date back to the seventh century. The word *Dunbeath* comes from Gaelic and means 'Fort of the Birches', conjuring up a time in the settlement's past when the area was prolific with birch trees.

Two vastly disparate deaths are recorded near the site of Dunbeath: in 1942, the forty-year-old Duke of Kent died in a tragic aircrash which happened just a few miles from the castle; and, three and a half centuries ago, the last wolf in Sutherland was killed, this is attested by an inscribed stone at the side of the road.

Ruins of Girnigeo and Sinclair Castles
CAITHNESS

It is difficult to tell where the cliff ends and the castles begin in this spectacular image of Caithness coastline. The ruins and the rocks blend in perfect harmony to create a landscape of unsurpassed grandeur. Sinclair and Girnigeo Castles have been ruined for centuries, but it is easy to see why they were built in such a place. The superb vantage point gained from the cliff-top position would have been invaluable in the days when invasions from Scandinavia were a constant concern in Caithness. However, despite the omnipresent image of the Norsemen as warmongering Vikings, the first Norse invaders to arrive in Caithness were peaceful peasants looking to begin a new life in less harsh conditions than those in their homeland.

Caithness stone has been imported throughout the world and can be found throughout Europe and on the other side of the globe. The Caithness district is full of fences dividing land into areas of ownership, created from the distinctive stone; the same stone was deemed perfect for paving slabs and, at the height of the Industrial Revolution, was richly sought after by urban architects. The pavements of opulent nineteenth-century cities, such as London, Paris and Melbourne were invariably created from the Scottish stone.

Haggs Castle
POLLOK GLASGOW

Haggs Castle, situated in Pollok Country Park, was built in 1585 by Sir John Maxwell of Pollok. The L-shaped, three-storey building is a perfect example of fortalice architecture, the style of building a small fort or creating a non-defensive building which looks like a fort.

In 1753, the building, in great need of repair, was abandoned by the Maxwell family. No money for the repairs, or a buyer for the castle, could be found and the once-stately home slowly descended into lonely ruins. In the nineteenth-century, Glasgow triumphed from the Industrial Revolution. The mills, factories and shipyards had never been more prosperous and many of the city's inhabitants were newly wealthy. In 1860, Haggs Castle was bought, restored and lived in once more.

During the Second World War, the castle became an important centre for army intelligence, and from then on has experienced a wide range of occupants. After the war, a developer turned the castle into flats, making it the second-oldest building in Glasgow to be still inhabited. In 1972, Haggs Castle became Glasgow's Museum of Childhood, sadly this was closed, due to council cutbacks, in 1996. Today the castle's future is uncertain once more.

Dunrobin Castle
NEAR GOLSPIE SUTHERLAND

Dunrobin, Scotland's most northerly castle, was the seat of the Earls and Dukes of Sutherland. The building, whose architecture has a strong French influence, has a grand total of 189 rooms and is renowned for being the largest house in the northern Highlands. Its illustrious history dates back to the fourteenth century.

The county of Sutherland was named by the Vikings. The word means 'southern land' and could only have been deemed a suitable name by people from a country as northerly as those of Scandinavia. The aristocratic families of Sutherland and Caithness, whose lands border one another, have a long history of rivalry. In 1567, the Earl and Countess of Sutherland were poisoned, by the grasping Earl of Caithness, who was desperate to secure the lands of Sutherland and enjoin them with his own. After the death of his parents, the fifteen-year-old son of the hapless Sutherlands was forced into marriage with the thirty-two-year old daughter of the Earl of Caithness.

Palace of Holyroodhouse
EDINBURGH

The Palace of Holyroodhouse (also called Holyrood Palace) is the British monarch's official residence in Scotland. This magnificent building is sited at the end of Edinburgh's Royal Mile, at the opposite end from Edinburgh Castle, and beneath the lowering splendour of Arthur's Seat. The palace's site was originally chosen by King David I in 1128. According to legend, he saw a miraculous 'rood' (a cross) materialise between the locked antlers of two fighting stags. As a result of this vision, he built an abbey and called it Holyrood.

Holyrood Palace was built in *c.* 1500 and has been a home to royalty since King James IV (1488–1513). This picture shows the grand entrance, complete with the royal coat of arms above the doors; the row of emblems above the column height are thistles, the emblem of Scotland.

Mary, Queen of Scots spent six years living at Holyrood palace. She arrived from France as a young widow in 1561 and the palace witnessed both her following two marriages – to Lord Darnley and Earl Bothwell –and the death of her favourite secretary, David Rizzio. On 9 March 1566, Rizzio was brutally murdered in front of the horrified Mary by a jealous Lord Darnley; in turn, Darnley was later murdered by Bothwell.

Craignethan Castle
CROSSFORD CLYDESDALE STRATHCLYDE

The remains of Craignethan Castle are sited in a small dell overlooking the River Nethan. There has been a castle here since at least the fifteenth century, when Craignethan was a Hamilton stronghold. At one time a proud, illustrious house, the castle suffered at the hands of the English after the defeat of Mary, Queen of Scots. The Hamilton family were staunch supporters of Mary and, as such, incurred the full strength of the English army's wrath.

Scotland has always been renowned for its spectacular array of grand homes. An account written in the thirteenth century stated that the country was abundant with over 120 castles, and this number did not take into account other important houses such as palaces and mansions. At that time, castles were not just the homes of royalty, they were also built to house the families of clan chiefs or wealthy merchants. Every person of high social status would have owned at least one castle, an illustrious family seat passed on through the male line to ensure it could never fall into the hands of a rival.

Dunstaffnage Castle
OBAN ARGYLLSHIRE

In the thirteenth century, the Scottish people and monarchy were under constant threat and actual attack from the Norwegians. Various castles were built towards the edge of the mainland to help stay the attacks, Dunstaffnage Castle was one such fortification. Alexander II (1214–1249) was one of the Scots kings whose reign was filled with the fear of a Norse invasion. He fought them, and won, early in his reign but in 1249 led a fatal second expedition. After a valiant battle, Alexander was mortally wounded and died at Kerrera, not far from Oban and Dunstaffnage Castle.

Robert the Bruce also had strong associations with Dunstaffnage Castle. After a series of disastrous battles and trials, in which he seemed to have lost everything, including his family, his luck finally started to take a turn for the better. After overthrowing his opposition in the north, he determined to conquer the west as well. Well-armed with a legion of supporters following his campaigning spirit into Argyllshire, Bruce managed to secure the assistance of the Mar and Ross families. In 1308 he claimed Dunstaffnage Castle, then the seat of the MacDougalls, and declared himself the fortress's master.

Floors Castle
NEAR KELSO THE BORDERS

Floors Castle stands alongside the River Tweed. It was built by William Adam in the 1720s and is the seat of the Duke of Roxburgh. The town of Roxburgh was created a royal burgh many centuries ago. As a strategically important centre the town was inevitably subjected to battles between the Scots and the English; similarly to Berwick-upon-Tweed, the inhabitants of the town alternated variously between being owned by Scotland and owned by England.

On one such memorable occasion, in 1460, the English occupants of the castle were being beseiged by the Scottish king, James II (1437–60). The battle was raging with cannons firing at the English-held Roxburgh Castle (now just a small pile of stones not far from the site of Floors Castle). One of the cannons had stopped working, creating a problem for James's tightly planned strategy. The king attempted to discover what was causing the problem but, as he was bending over the cannon to inspect it, the barrel exploded killing both the king and the Scots' dreams of taking Roxburgh.

The land upon which James died is now part of the gardens of Floors Castle. A yew tree was planted upon the fatal spot and still stands to this day.

View to Inverness Castle
INVERNESS-SHIRE

In AD 565, St Columba had arrived in Scotland from Ireland and had established a thriving Christian community. In the same year, he paid a visit to the King Brude, ruler of the Picts, in a peace-making mission between the old and the new cultures of Scotland. The site of the King's residence was a stronghold in Inverness. Although the first castle was not built until the twelfth century, there has been a fortress of some kind in Inverness since the time of King Brude, and probably beforehand.

Inverness Castle was built by King David I in *c.* 1140. This view of the splendid building was taken from the banks of the River Ness, on which the town of Inverness is sited. The river runs into the Caledonian Canal, and was essential to the district's trade before the invention of motorised travel. Inverness Castle gazes imperiously over the town from its vantage point on the river's bank.

In the early eighteenth century, the castle was occupied by Jacobite soldiers until it was blown up during the Forty-Five. The present, stately buildings that comprise the castle, in fact date only from the mid-nineteenth century.

Linlithgow Palace
LINLITHGOW WEST LOTHIAN

The site on which the ruined palace now stands was originally home to a hunting lodge, dating back to 1301. In 1424, Linlithgow Palace, family home to the royal Stuarts, was created from the lodge's foundations, but just two years later, the palace was razed to the ground by fire. The Stuarts rebuilt their home, a palace that, since that time, has seen many of history's most famous, and infamous, figures pass through its portals.

In 1542, the palace saw the birth of perhaps the most ill-fated monarch of all time, Mary, Queen of Scots; in later years, the palace has also been home to the occupying Oliver Cromwell; Bonnie Prince Charlie and, after the tragic Battle of Culloden, to the Duke of Cumberland. 'Butcher Cumberland' then burnt the palace down.

Since that time, the palace's stones have stood in silent testimony to a grand and grisly history for over two hundred years.

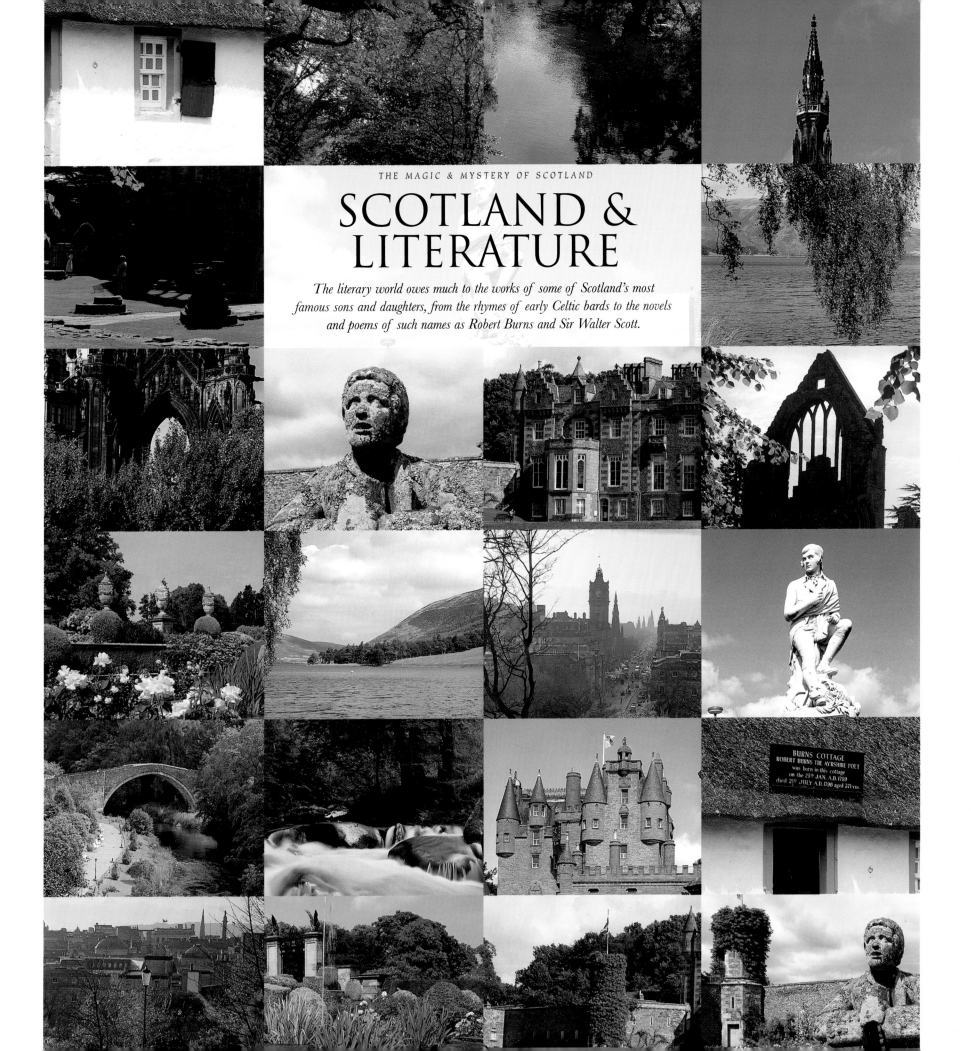

SCOTLAND & LITERATURE

The literary world owes much to the works of some of Scotland's most famous sons and daughters, from the rhymes of early Celtic bards to the novels and poems of such names as Robert Burns and Sir Walter Scott.

BURNS COTTAGE
ROBERT BURNS THE AYRSHIRE POET
was born in this cottage
on the 25TH JAN. A.D. 1759
died 21ST JULY A.D. 1796 aged 37½ yrs.

Scott Monument
EDINBURGH

This imposing monument dominates the skyline of Edinburgh from whatever direction the city is viewed. The size of the incredible edifice is indicative of Scott's importance to the people of Scotland, and to those of Edinburgh in particular. Sir Walter Scott was born in College Wynd, Edinburgh in 1771. He trained in law at Edinburgh University, but chose to pursue a literary career. The novelist's identity was kept a closely guarded secret for several years, being credited in his books purely as 'by the author of Waverley' and it was in Edinburgh, in the George Street Assembly Rooms, that his identity was first revealed. The revelation caused a sensation.

Scott's monument was designed by G. M. Kemp, and built between 1840 and 1844. Sadly Kemp died before his creation was finished. The staggeringly tall Gothic-style edifice is 220ft in height. Located on Edinburgh's main thoroughfare, Princes Street, it is an construction that no visitor to Edinburgh could possibly fail to notice. The enormous spire leads up from a canopy covering a statue of Scott himself, depicted with his dog. The figures were created by Steell. The monument's typically ornate Gothic decorations are imaginatively intertwined with characters from Scott's novels.

Garden of Abbotsford House
MELROSE THE BORDERS

The most important aspect of Sir Walter Scott's gardens at Abbotsford House is that the original plans were designed entirely by the writer himself. Scott's main passion aside from writing was gardening, especially the planting of trees. His prolific tree-planting schemes at Abbotsford began a trend, as a result, a great many grand houses now have fine avenues dating back to the time of Scott. The wall, which can be seen surrounding the garden in this photograph, was built from stone that Scott brought from his home town of Edinburgh; stones which came from Edinburgh's old market place.

Many of Scott's beloved trees were fruit trees, which he tended with great care. In an extraordinarily forward-thinking manner, Scott arranged heating to keep his fruit trees in a temperature at which they would flourish. He managed this by having a series of pipes installed, which ran through the surrounding walls and heated the orchard.

At the top of the garden is an orangerie; it was one of Scott's favourite places to be. Each evening, the distinguished writer would retire to his orangerie, listen to the strains of his piper, whose house stood just behind the wall, and say prayers for the well-being of his family.

Abbotsford House
MELROSE THE BORDERS

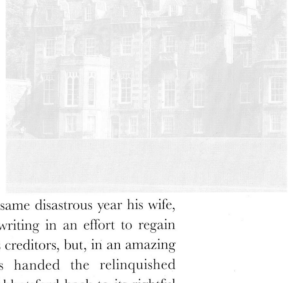

This grand house, impeccably situated on the banks of the River Tweed, was the home of Sir Walter Scott. The original building on the site was a simple farmhouse named Cartleyhole, which Scott bought in 1811. Scott tore down the farmhouse to build a grand design of his own devising, which was completed in 1822. He named the house Abbotsford after discovering that the monks of Melrose Abbey used to use this spot to cross the river.

In 1826, the publishing business in which Scott was a partner went bankrupt. Scott incurred huge debts as a result and lost everything, including his home. In the same disastrous year his wife, Margaret, died. Scott threw himself into writing in an effort to regain some of his lost fortune and to pay back his creditors, but, in an amazing display of selflessness, Scott's creditors handed the relinquished Abbotsford back to its rightful owner before he had finished paying them back.

Scott had a passion for collecting historic relics and Abbotsford still houses a great many of these. He amassed such artefacts as Rob Roy's gun, Bonnie Prince Charlie's drinking bowl and the Duke of Montrose's sword. His vivid imagination helped transform these objects into colourful additions to his novels.

Dryburgh Abbey
DRYBURGH THE BORDERS

The site of Dryburgh Abbey has been consecrated ground since the sixth century; at that time it housed the sanctuary of an Irish holyman who has become known as St Modan. Six centuries later, in 1150, the first abbey, a monastery, was founded on the site of St Modan's sanctuary.

The abbey has a chequered architectural history, having been destroyed and rebuilt several times since the fourteenth century – always by the English. In 1322 and 1385, the stones were razed to the ground and the abbey recreated; in 1544 the English decimated the building for the third and final time. It has never been rebuilt. However, the destruction was not entire, and in spite of its ruined state, the abbey still remains a wonderful example of twelfth- and thirteenth-century religious life.

Today the abbey is best known as the last resting place of the great novelist Sir Walter Scott. Scott's family were once the owners of the land on which the abbey stood, and fell, but in the eighteenth century the family's rights of ownership dwindled until all that was left was the simple, ancient licence of being allowed to be buried there.

The Gardens of Manderston House
NEAR DUNS THE BORDERS

Berwickshire was one of Robert Louis Stevenson's favourite regions and many of his stories were based around this area; his childhood home in North Berwick is said to have inspired the setting for his world-famous pirate novel *Treasure Island*.

Stevenson spent much of his time travelling from his home town of Edinburgh absorbing the narrative inspirations of Scotland and honing his impeccable skill of story-telling. One such story tells of when he visited the south-western province of Ayrshire: the people reputedly threw stones at him in the street, because of his city clothes, unseen before in that part of the country.

Manderston House, of which the sumptuous gardens are shown here, is a splendid example of fine country living. The house belonged to Sir James Millar, a wealthy man who had inherited a fortune from trading with Russia in hemp and herrings. Sir James returned to Scotland as a Boer War veteran determined to pursue a gentler pastime. Together with the notable architect John Kinross, Millar transformed his house and gardens. Manderston's gardens, combining the formal and informal areas, encompass fifty-six acres of land.

West Shore of St Mary's Loch
THE BORDERS

The works of Sir Walter Scott drew inspiration from many and varied areas of Scotland and, like Robbie Burns, one can find memorials to the great novelist and poet throughout the country.

Scott's work was romantic and chivalrous, redolent of a bygone age and evocative of the beautiful scenery of his homeland. His novels include *Rob Roy, The Heart of Midlothian, Perveril of the Peak* and *Ivanhoe*. He also wrote a great many poems, such as 'The Lady of the Lake', 'Harold the Dauntless' and, perhaps his most famous, 'Lochinvar', an epic romantic poem set in the heart of his beloved Border Country:

> *O young Lochinvar is come out of the west,*
> *Through all the wide Border his steed was the best;*
> *And save his good broadsword he weapons had none,*
> *He rode all unarm'd, and he rode all alone.*
> *So faithful in love, and so dauntless in war,*
> *There never was knight like the young Lochinvar.*
>
> **Sir Walter Scott**

Scott was one of Scotland's most prolific ambassadors and an important peacemaker between England and Scotland. It was he who introduced the formal, pleated kilt as appropriate wear, to mark the visit to Scotland by King George IV. Much of the outer world's vision of Scotland today comes from Scott's promotion of his country.

View from Calton Hill
EDINBURGH

Here the city of Edinburgh, framed by a brilliantly sharp sunset, shows the home of Robert Louis Stevenson's literary inspiration in all its glory. Stunning in the rich colours of an autumn sunset, one can imagine how eerie the same image could look if shrouded in darkness. On a foggy night this could easily be a haunt of Dr Jekyll's alter ego, Mr Hyde. Stevenson is one of Edinburgh's most stalwart literary figures. His name and those of his characters can be found throughout the city: in the areas he visited, in the names of pubs re-christened to reflect his influence and in the history recreated in his masterpieces.

The Strange Case of Dr Jekyll and Mr Hyde is one of Stevenson's best-known works; an incredible novel, gripping in content and compellingly written. The story of a respectable scientist who turns into an evil, blood-chillingly vicious figure was based on a real Edinburgh character, Deacon Brodie. A well-respected pillar of eighteenth-century society, Deacon Brodie had a far more sinister side. His exploits include robbery and murder, yet he remained unsuspected for decades. When finally caught, tried and hanged for his crimes, the discovery shocked Edinburgh to its core. In an irony worthy of a Stevenson plot, Deacon Brodie was hanged using a mechanism of which he was the inventor.

Robert Burns Statue
DUMFRIES DUMFRIESSHIRE

Should auld acquaintance be forgot
And never brought to mind?
Should auld acquaintance be forgot,
And auld lang syne!

Robert Burns

This romantic statue of Burns stands in the town where he ended his days, at the tender age of thirty-seven. The memory of Robert Burns is one that will never fade. Not just because of his wonderful poetry, but also due to the many statues and memorials standing in testimony to his literary greatness, and because of the enthusiasm with which his memory is kept alive through annual Burns Nights festivities. These take place on or around his birth date, 25 January, wherever there are Scots throughout the globe.

Burns moved to Dumfries in 1791 and stayed there for the rest of his short life. He wrote many of his most celebrated poems here, including, probably, his best-known work: 'Auld Land Syne'. His house in Dumfries has been turned into a museum and its location, formerly known as Mill Vennel, is now called Burns Street. Although Robbie died in 1796, his wife, Jean (née Armour) lived here until her death in 1834.

Old Brig o' Doon

ALLOWAY AYRSHIRE

The thirteenth-century Brig o' Doon, was brought to life in Robert Burns' poem 'Tam o' Shanter'. It is the bridge over which Tam and his horse Meg just manage to escape – minus Meg's tail – when pursued by witches, a feat realised because witches cannot cross water. Also mentioned in 'Tam o' Shanter' is the Auld Kirkyard in Alloway, the place where the witches and warlocks dance, and the ale-house in Alloway square, now fittingly renamed 'The Tam o' Shanter'.

Ah, Tam! Ah, Tam! thou'll get thy fairin!
In hell they'll roast thee like a herrin!
... Now, do thy speedy utmost, Meg,
And win the key-stane of the brig;
There at them thou thy tail may toss,
A running stream they dare na cross.
Robert Burns

In 1823, a monument was erected to the memory of Burns, not far from the Brig o' Doon. It was built in the unlikely form of a Grecian temple by Thomas Hamilton, one of Scotland's premier architects and an afficionado of Burns' literature. Hamilton made a copy of this monument, which he replicated at the top of Edinburgh's Calton Hill.

Waterfall at Aberfeldy
PERTHSHIRE

The area around Aberfeldy was immortalised by Robbie Burns in his wonderfully evocative poem the 'Birks of Aberfeldy'. The word *birk* means 'silver birch', and Burns' poem is about these trees, which so effortlessly and elegantly line the Urlar Burn. This picturesque waterfall was created from the bubbling current of the birch trees' river; the lush greenery of the leaves and mossy stones, the clear sky glimpsed through the laden branches and the misty hues of the rushing water perfectly recreate the image captured by the poet.

Now simmer blinks on flowery braes,
And o'er the crystal streamlet plays
Come let us spend the lightsome days
In the Birks of Aberfeldy.

The little birdies blythely sing,
While o'er their heads the hazels hing
Or lightly flit on wanton wing
In the Birks of Aberfeldy.

The braes ascend like lofty wa's,
The foaming stream deep-roaring fa's
O'erhung wi' fragrant spreading shaws –
The Birks of Aberfeldy

Robert Burns

Side View of Glamis Castle
ANGUS

There has been a building on this site for over 1000 years. Parts of the present castle date back to the fourteenth century and some of the oldest walls are fifteen feet wide. Glamis Castle is the home of the Queen Mother, and Princess Margaret was born here.

The antihero of William Shakespeare's *Macbeth* is the Thane of Glamis, and, although it is never mentioned by name, Glamis Castle is the place Shakespeare intended for the setting, and of here that Duncan makes the speech,

> *This castle has a pleasant seat; the air*
> *Nimbly and sweetly recommends itself*
> *Unto our gentle senses.*
>
> **William Shakespeare**

There is a room in the castle now named Duncan's Hall, but there is no documentary evidence that the real Macbeth ever visited here. Nor was he such a sinister figure as Shakespeare suggests. He, and his wife, did murder Duncan, but Duncan was not the good, noble king portrayed in the play and Macbeth had equal claim to the throne. Macbeth killed Duncan in 1040, then reigned until he was killed by Duncan's son, Malcolm, in 1057.

Burns' Cottage
ALLOWAY AYRSHIRE

Robert Burns was born on 25 January 1759, to a farmer, William Burnes, and his wife. The couple, who changed their names to Burns while Robbie was a lad, had moved to Ayrshire from their homeland of Kincardineshire. Burns has become revered as the most famous poet in Scot's history and no one can visit the land of his birth without seeing his name scattered liberally about – on pub names, bookshops and museums. Lesser known, however, is the fact that he also re-arranged many of Scotland's traditional folk songs. When Burns died in 1796, he left behind him a nation in mourning, but also a nation enhanced by the richness of his poetry: poems in their own language, not the pronunciation of a foreign tongue.

Robbie's parents had acquired land in Alloway, three miles from the town of Ayr. On this site stood a simple clay hut, which his father tore down and replaced with the larger thatched cottage seen in this photograph; it was finished in 1757. Nearby are many places immortalised in Burns' works, including the Brig o' Doon, Alloway Kirk, the Auld Brig and the Auld Kirkyard. Today Burns' cottage is a museum celebrating the life of its son.

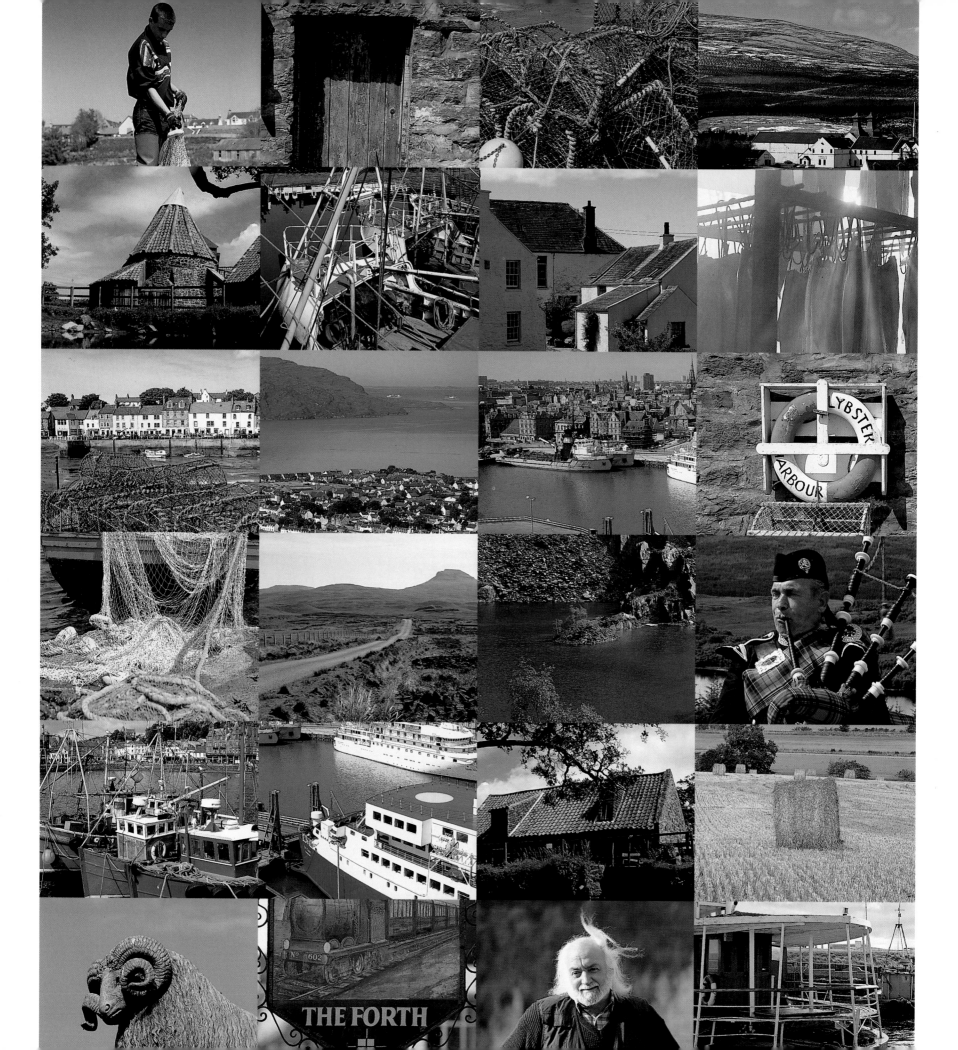

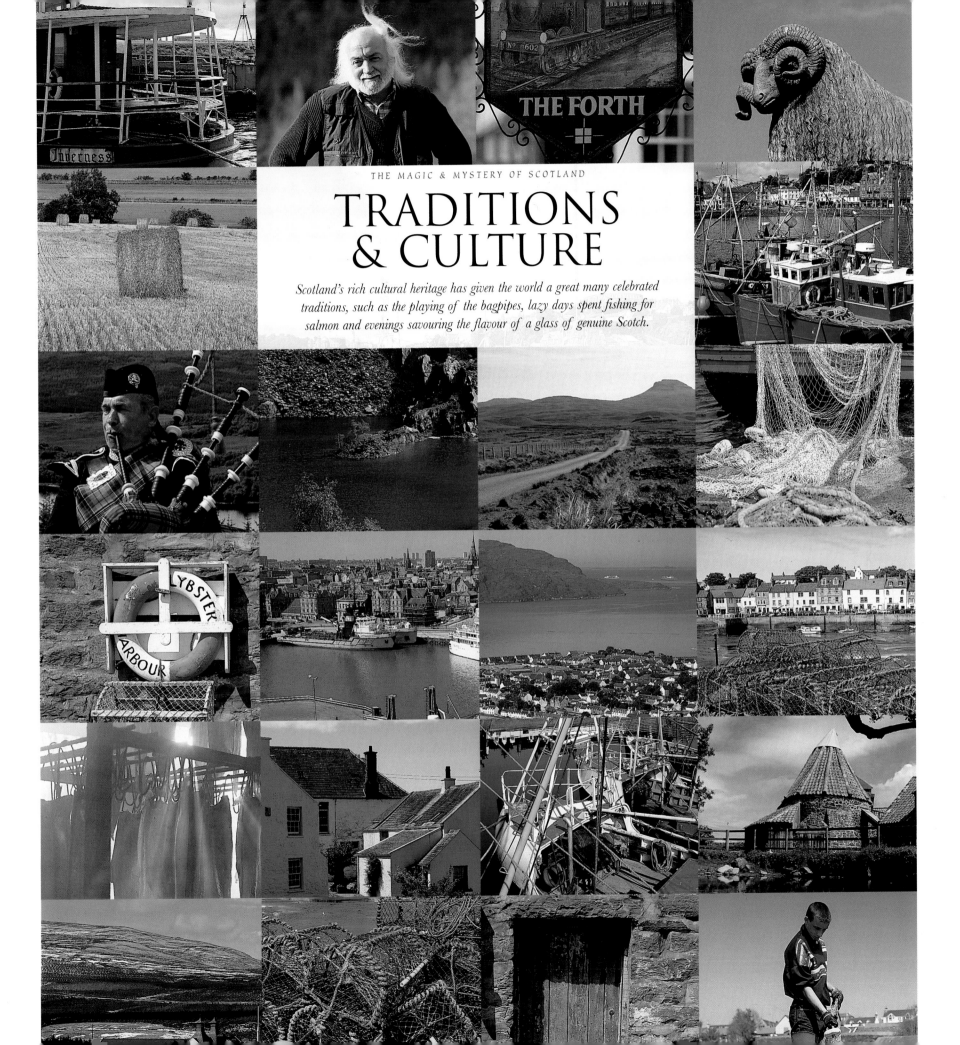

THE MAGIC & MYSTERY OF SCOTLAND

TRADITIONS & CULTURE

Scotland's rich cultural heritage has given the world a great many celebrated traditions, such as the playing of the bagpipes, lazy days spent fishing for salmon and evenings savouring the flavour of a glass of genuine Scotch.

Playing The Bagpipes
LOCH GARRY INVERNESS-SHIRE

The bagpipes are one of the most evocative images of Celtic culture. Their omnipresent, haunting sound pervades the air of Scotland, linking past and present in a common strain.

Invergarry, near the spot where this piper stands, played an important, and bloody, part in Scots history. It was here, in Invergarry Castle, that the MacDonells hid the Young Pretender, both before and after Culloden. In an act illustrative of his nickname, 'Butcher Cumberland' instructed his Hanoverian forces to burn down the castle in retribution for the MacDonells' loyalty to the prince. Today all that can be seen are the castle walls, still standing in defiance.

After the turbulence of the Forty-Five, the English government attempted to remove all traces of Gaelic culture, fearing that its continuance would serve to preserve the warriors' cause. By eliminating their culture, the English hoped to subjugate the Celtic soul. As a result, wearing tartan and playing the bagpipes were forbidden throughout Scotland for many decades.

Ballachulish
LOCH LEVEN ARGYLLSHIRE

The history of Ballachulish's slate industry dates back to as long ago as the seventeenth century. In 1693, a community of travelling workers arrived in Ballachulish. They were skilled labourers with a wide knowledge of Scotland and her landscapes and, after surveying the local area they recognised the surrounding stone as slate – an industry was born.

Over the next century, groups of people began moving to the area, attracted by the reputation of the works and the money to be made. By 1791, a small town had been established, the population of which numbered over 300. At the start of the nineteenth century, slate from Ballachulish was being used to roof houses throughout the whole of Scotland, as well as being imported further afield.

With the quarry's prime location, encircling the waters of Loch Leven, the works had immediate access to vital waterways needed to transport the stone. The Ballachulish slate industry flourished for over two and a half centuries, sadly closing down in 1955.

Peat Blocks
NEAR DUNVEGAN SKYE INNER HEBRIDES

The discovery of peat and its benefits to society created an important industry on the Isle of Skye. Seen here are blocks of peat left to dry until hard. The processing of peat is arduous, manual labour that demands thorough knowledge and skill. At the start, the peat workers cut away the surface vegetation from the bog and remove a first layer of peat. This is cut into strips, then blocks, and laid out to dry. Each block is turned over several times to ensure that it dries all the way through. When Dr Samuel Johnson visited Scotland during the eighteenth century, he wrote that he had experienced two firsts: he had heard the Celtic language and seen (and smelled!) fires made from peat.

The Dunvegan area is the home of the Clan McLeod. According to legend, the clan's fourth chief was given a magic flag by his wife, who was a fairy. After giving him the flag, she disappeared into McLeod's Tables – the hills which can be seen in this photograph – and was never seen again. The flag is said to bring the McLeods luck in battle, to ensure an heir for the chief and to bring herrings into the loch so the clan will never go hungry.

Bonar Bridge
DORNOCH FIRTH SUTHERLAND

Fishing was the reason most coastal villages in Scotland were created. It was the lifeblood of a small community and the seas of Scotland are still renowned for the quality of their fish. The fishermen in this photograph are seen gathering their nets in preparation for a hard day's fishing in the waters near Bonar Bridge, North-East Scotland. Bonar Bridge marks the traditional spot for pilgrims making their way to Tain, a sacred centre of Christianity for many hundreds of years. Among the many visitors to Tain was Robert the Bruce in the fourteenth century.

Dornoch is abundant with seals, who vye with the fishers for the best catch of the day. Both common and grey seals can be found in Scotland's waters and whales (Pilot Whales, Minke Whales and even the occasional Orca), dolphins, and porpoises can often be seen from the shore. Dornoch also has a place in Scotland's more gory history. It was the site of the last official witch-burning. The witch of Dornoch was a woman accused of pacts with the devil and performing spells: according to the accusers she transformed her daughter into a pony, and allowed the Devil to shoe her.

Lybster Harbour
CAITHNESS COAST CAITHNESS

This picture shows a harbour cottage in Lybster, a small, ancient harbour town, on one of Scotland's most remote northern coasts. Outside the cottage rest a plethora of lobster pots, emphasising the community's dependence on the fishing industry, and a life-saving ring – the sea around this area of Scotland is very, very cold and can be extremely turbulent.

The shore that rims Caithness brims with fascinating history, it is the kind of place from which legends drip. Travelling along the coast, one can see the standing stones at Achanavich, a convergence of ancient burial cairns, and the Hill o'Many Stanes, an ancient monument, comprising over 200 carefully arranged stones, dating from the Bronze Age. As well as its Bronze Age settlement, Lybster is known to have been a home to Norse invaders – the town's name comes from the Norse language, echoing a history of Viking settlers – and a Celtic community, represented by the presence of a carved Celtic high cross.

Aberdeen Harbour

ABERDEENSHIRE

The picturesque city of Aberdeen has been a popular settlement since prehistoric times. The waters of the River Dee and the sea into which it flows, provided an abundance of fish to feed the communities of the Stone and Bronze Ages and their successors – Picts, Celts and the ever-hopeful Romans.

Aberdeen harbour is formed by the mouth of the River Dee, which provides a plentiful source of income for its fisheries and, in the twentieth century, has created exploration opportunities for fossil fuel companies.

Aberdeen has received much attention from Scotland's famous and notorious. King William the Lion created it a royal burgh in the twelfth century; Robert the Bruce hid from his English pursuers in a safe house within the town; and Butcher Cumberland resided here in splendour while waiting for the offensive from the Jacobite army – which led to the Battle of Culloden. Aberdeen is also famous for its university, which in 1641, received the Royal charter from the luckless King Charles I.

Port of Ullapool
LOCH BROOM INVERNESS-SHIRE

This panoramic view of the eighteenth-century port of Ullapool, sited on the north-east shore of Loch Broom shows Ben Goleach in the distance. Loch Broom is noted for the exceptional beauty of the flora and fauna which inhabit its shores.

Not far from Ullapool lies the breath-taking spectacle of the Corrieshalloch Gorge. The grandiose beauty of the gorge is due mainly to its great size: it is a mile long and drops down to the awe-inspiring depth of 200ft. The turbulent waters plunge their way down the Falls of Measach, providing an incredible view.

A few miles outside Ullapool is the abandoned village of Badbea – most of the town's original inhabitants emigrated to New Zealand to start a life less hard than the one they knew. Having been cleared from their earlier homes by a grasping landlord, the villagers had to battle their way through life in one of the world's most windy areas. Children and animals had to be tethered to strong trees and buildings to stop them being blown off the cliffs. Today there is a monument to honour those who lived here.

Anstruther Harbour
FIFE PENINSULA

At the start of this century, Anstruther harbour was one of Scotland's richest fishing ports, the epicentre of the lucrative herring fishing industry. Unfortunately, in the 1940s, herring began to disappear from the waters around Fife and the wealth of Anstruther's fisheries began to trickle away.

An ancient settlement, Anstruther is associated with many legends from times gone by. One such legend concerns the nearby island of May, and the body of a ninth-century saint. It is said that St Adrian was murdered by Vikings when they attacked his island. His body was laid to rest in the ground of May. However, one morning when the local fishermen were starting their day's work from Anstruther harbour, they saw a large object floating towards them. When the object reached the shore, it was discovered to be a stone coffin, containing the still intact remains of St Adrian. To this day, the saint's remains are said to lie in the cemetery of the local church.

Smoking The Salmon
INVERAWE SMOKERY ARGYLLSHIRE

For many of Scotland's myriad tourists the lure is not the mountains of the Highlands, the solitude of deserted silver-sanded beaches or the glorious architecture of the cities; it is not the purple heather, the frenzied colours of Edinburgh's Fringe Festival nor even the glistening gold of a tumbler full of Scotch whisky. For these tourists, the ultimate goal of a Scottish holiday is the peace of the lochs, the swish of a fishing line and the chance to net one of Scotland's famed pink salmon.

Salmon are almost a national emblem of Scotland. Throughout the centuries they have been an important source of wealth in areas of abundance. Before 1800, salmon were salted and pickled before exportation, however the art of smoking became a very popular one in the nineteenth century and revolutionised the Scotch salmon industry. Exclusive restaurants, society parties, exquisite delicatessans and the abundantly stocked food halls of the most expensive stores in the world would be nothing without Scottish smoked salmon.

Harbour Cottage and Galley
KIRKCUDBRIGHT SOLWAY FIRTH LOTHIAN

The Solway Firth holds an important part of Scotland's history in its grasp, for it was here that the western side of Hadrian's Wall began, built by the Roman Emperor Hadrian to separate the land he controlled from the land he never could.

The Romans first arrived in Britain around 55 BC, on an investigative expedition; by AD 43 their aim was to take over the entire island. After fierce territorial battles, the tribes of England and Wales eventually succumbed to the brute force and military power of the sophisticated Roman Empire, but the Picts and Celts of the land now called Scotland, refused to bow down in suppression.

Several towns in Scotland still bear the remains of Roman fortifications, Edinburgh, Glasgow and Perth to name just three, but these were purely defensive as control of the land proved too impossible. In AD

122, the Roman forces admitted defeat, realising they would never be able to tame the ferocity of the warrior tribes. In a decisive gesture, Hadrian's forces built a bridge spanning the island from the Solway in the west to the Tyne in the east. Today, this picturesque harbour remains on the site of the Roman Empire's symbol of failure.

Morning scene at Ullapool
INVERNESS-SHIRE

The fishing town of Ullapool was founded by the British Fisheries Society in 1788. For many years it enjoyed a thriving industry exporting herrings throughout the world, but, sadly, today the visitor to Ullapool is more likely to see the all-too familiar sight of European factory ships, than Scots herring boats. Fishing is of vital importance to small communities such as this one, it is a trade that goes back to the beginning of time, but one that the Scots are having fiercely to defend against the onslaught of a new European parliament.

Ullapool is surrounded by natural beauty spots: twelve miles to the north is the Inverapolly Nature Reserve; twelve miles to the south is a suspension bridge. This bridge spans the Corrieshalloch Gorge and the Falls of Measach and, from the perfect vantage point that the bridge affords, one can gaze at the magnificent spectacle of one hundred and fifty feet of rushing water plunging down to the bowl of the gorge.

Preston Mill
EAST LINTON EAST LOTHIAN

The mill buildings at East Linton date from the sixteenth century, making it one of Scotland's oldest water-mills still working today. Its East Lothian site, beside this peaceful, undulating river, has been home to a mill since the thirteenth century. The mills in this area were primarily used for grinding oatmeal, an essential part of the Scotch diet and vital for animal fodder. Every oatmeal mill would have two buildings: the mill, which processed the grain, and a kiln for drying it.

In the sixteenth century, the land of East Linton and much of the surrounding area was owned by the Hepburns, a hugely influential aristocratic family, of which the husband of Mary, Queen of Scots was a member. In later years, the land was sold to the Grays who still own much of it today.

Close to Preston Mill was a mill owned by the Meikle brothers, the engineering pioneers who invented threshing machines. One of their apprentices was a certain John Rennie. The Meikle brothers' young apprentice went on to be one of the best known names in the engineering world to this day, famed for his marsh draining projects (including the Solway marshes) and his construction of harbours and bridges (including London's Waterloo Bridge).

Black Isle
ROSS AND CROMARTY INVERNESS-SHIRE

The Black Isle in the area of Ross and Cromarty is neither an island nor is it black. Instead it is a green and fertile peninsular of the mainland which, as can be seen here, enjoys some of the best farming country in the land. The reason for its being known as an island is a mystery, but the origin of the word 'black' is less mysterious. Residents believe that it comes from the Gaelic word 'dubh', which, in turn, is a corruption of 'Duthac'. St Duthac was honoured by a shrine based at Tain, not far from the Black Isle, and his devoted pilgrims passed regularly through this area.

Before the seventeenth century, Cromarty was one of Scotland's most prosperous and lively ports. Remains of the grand houses still stand, alongside fishing cottages. Cromarty was also home to the eminent geologist Hugh Miller, who lived here in the nineteenth century. As well as being a geologist, Miller was a strong Christian and prolific writer. He published a revolutionary paper on an anti-evolutionary interpretation of fossils.

Railway Pier
OBAN ARGYLLSHIRE

Oban, a lively town with a population of around 8500, is also known as 'the gateway to the islands' because of the ease with which one can reach the Hebrides, particularly the Isle of Mull. This colourful scene shows a wonderful array of freshly painted fishing boats tied to the railway pier in the town's harbour.

Oban had its heyday in the nineteenth century when it was a very popular holiday resort. In 1897 a typically Victorian folly was built here by a banker named John McCaig. In true nineteenth-century style, he chose a replica of a central piece of world architecture – in this case the Colosseum of Rome. The folly was built as a memorial to his family and as a philanthropic gesture: McCaig knew that its construction would provide work for local labourers. The folly is sited at the summit of the town's tallest hill, a steep climb for which the walker is rewarded on arrival by the breathtaking views of the Isle of Mull.

Scotland's Most Northerly Harbour
JOHN O' GROATS CAITHNESS

This may be Scotland's most northerly harbour but, contrary to popular belief, John O'Groats is *not* Scotland's most northerly point. Dunnet Head has that distinction. Since records began, John O' Groats has been acclaimed as the furthest north point on the British mainland – except by the Greek astronomer Ptolemy, who made the first reference to Dunnet Head being Scotland's northernmost spot.

John O'Groats was named after a sixteenth-century Dutch explorer, Jan de Groot. De Groot arrived in Scotland, at the point that now bears his name, and settled here.

Not far from John O'Groats is a steep, stone staircase of 365 steps, winding down a sheer cliff to Whaligoe Harbour. The steps are

treacherous and can be lethal in wet or icy weather. As a result few people risk using them. However, until recently, the stairs were lovingly cared for by a Caithness resident. She tended the stairway regularly, ensuring that the pass was kept clear and in good repair. Her motive for doing so was a fervent belief that Jesus, being a fisherman, would one day arrive at the coast of Caithness and she wanted the steps to be ready for him to climb.

Moffat
THE BORDERS DUMFRIESSHIRE

This bronze ram looks down on Scotland's widest High Street in the town of Moffat. The statue is symbolic of the Dumfriesshire community's past, present and future sheep-farming industry; an industry of which Moffat is at the centre. The history of Scotland's sheep farming industry, however, has not always been a happy one. Up in the Highlands, thousands of people were forced out of their homes and villages to make way for sheep. The land was cleared of humans and made suitable for grazing. This has become known as the 'Clearances' and took place in the eighteenth and nineteenth centuries.

As well as its thriving sheep-farming community, Moffat also has a history of another lucrative trade: in the seventeenth century, Moffat was famed as a spa town and prized for the healing powers of its waters. Wealthy invalids travelled to the small Borders town in the hopes that its curative waters would prove effective. The townspeople began a thriving hospitality business for the influx of tourists wishing to 'take the waters'.

Strathmashie
NEAR LAGGAN INVERNESS-SHIRE

Highlander Jim MacDonald is seen here in his everyday wear including a kilt and sporran. The wearing of kilts extends back through many centuries and many cultures. Kilt-type garments were worn by the ancient Egyptians, Greeks and Romans as well as by tribes throughout Africa and Asia.

The first Highlanders wore plaids. These were lengths of tartan material, roughly about sixteen yards in length, although the amount varied according to social status. The plaid would have been put on in the following manner: first it would be laid flat on the ground, then gathered into folds. When the pleating was complete, the Highlander would pass his belt underneath it, roughly in the middle. After this preparation, he would lie down on the plaid, gather it around himself as many times as it would go and secure the belt. The extra material was worn over the shoulder serving in a variety of different functions: as a sleeping rug, tied as a pocket or wrapped around for extra warmth.

The Forth Inn
FIRTH OF FORTH WEST LOTHIAN

The Firth of Forth is sited just outside Edinburgh. This pub sign is a famous landmark for all those embarking from their boats after a hard day's fishing or sailing. Pubs in Scotland are an important part of the social scene.

Music can often be heard in pubs throughout Scotland. Celtic music has enjoyed a spectacular revival in the last few years and often one can enter the bar to the strains of a fiddle and the ambient sounds of a Gaelic song. The cross-over between Scottish and Irish culture may well be nowhere more apparent than in the warmth of a pub.

During Edinburgh's annual Festival of the arts, in combination with its parallel Fringe Festival, it can be a battle of brute force even to make it through the door of a pub in this area, as the population of the town and surrounding suburbs swells to twice its normal size. Likewise, throughout Scotland on New Year's Eve, or more correctly Hogmanay, the pub is a hive of activity and the heart of a community, whether in a city or village.

Dalwhinnie Distillery
DALWHINNIE INVERNESS-SHIRE

Dalwhinnie is possibly the highest village in Britain and definitely home to the world's highest distillery. The first Scottish distillery is reputed to have been sited in the Black Isle, in Ross and Cromarty. It was called the Ferintosh, and sadly no trace of it remains.

The word 'whisky' comes from the Gaelic 'uisge-beatha' meaning 'the water of life'. The art of whisky making has a great deal to do with water and the Scots claim there is no finer water throughout the world suited to whisky-making than that found in Scotland. For that reason distilleries are usually to be found near clear, natural water courses: tumbling streams and smooth-flowing rivers. Distilleries are often a central part of a farming comunity, which provides the distillers with all they need.

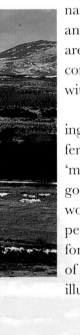

Whisky is made from just three ingredients: water, yeast and barley. It is fermented in gleaming copper tubs, called 'mash tuns' and distilled into the clear, golden liquid known throughout the world simply as 'Scotch'. For many people, 'Scotch' is a generic word for whisky, but only the true whisky of Scotland can lay claim to the illustrious title.

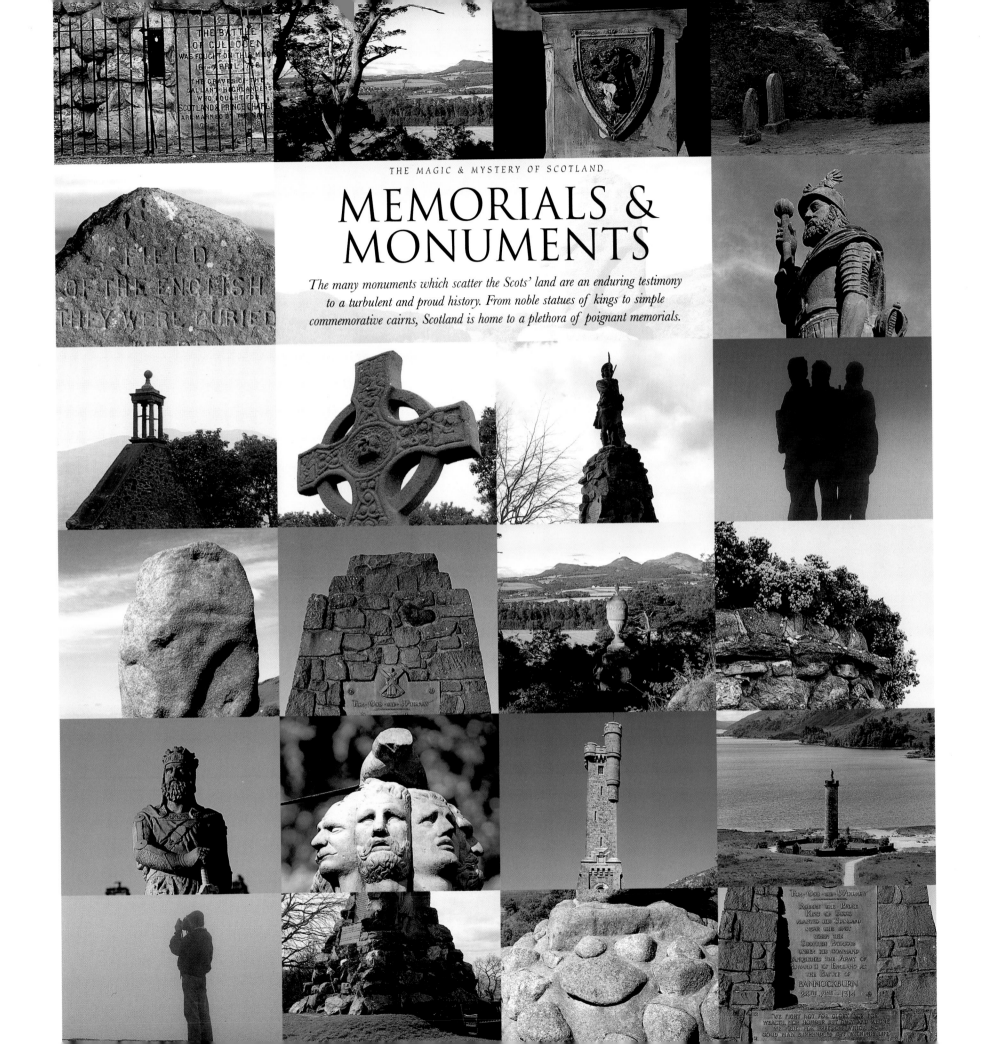

MEMORIALS & MONUMENTS

The many monuments which scatter the Scots' land are an enduring testimony to a turbulent and proud history. From noble statues of kings to simple commemorative cairns, Scotland is home to a plethora of poignant memorials.

Balquhidder Church
BALQUHIDDER STIRLING REGION

Within the cemetery of Balquhidder Church lies a legend – the graves of Robert Roy MacGregor, together with those of his wife and two sons. A charismatic figure, Rob Roy is remembered diversely as Scotland's greatest fugitive outlaw, hero and thief. The story and vitality of his life has inspired scribes ranging from Sir Walter Scott to Hollywood script-writers. His name has become synonymous with Scotland's fight against the constraints of English rule. Rob Roy was born in 1671, in the region of Loch Lomond. He married a fellow MacGregor, Helen, with whom he had two sons – Coll and Robert. Rob Roy died in 1734, survived by all his family, although Coll died just one year after his father.

The stones adorning the graves in Balquhidder church-yard are unnamed, but bear pictorial honours to a family re-united in death. One stone bears the arms of the Clan MacGregor, another a carving of a Highlander, proudly resplendent in traditional plaid.

Kildalton Cross
KILDALTON ISLAY INNER HEBRIDES

Kildalton's outstanding cross is believed to be the work of a sculptor who hailed from nearby Iona. The cross was intricately carved, from local stone, in the ninth century, but the reason for its creation is unknown.

Islay was, like many of Scotland's islands, home to a fervently religious community of Celtic Christians, a spirituality that has remained throughout the centuries. In the eighteenth century the town of Bowmore, now Islay's capital, was founded. The focal point of the town is the church, sited at the top of the hill to look down upon its congregation in their homes. The church is a spectacular architectural achievement and the most fascinating aspect of its building is its round shape. According to legend, the builders constructed it in this way so that there would be corners for the devil to hide in. Bowmore also made history by being the first village in Scotland to be constructed according to a plan.

Black Watch Monument
ABERFELDY PERTHSHIRE

In 1667, the second Duke of Atholl and several other clan chiefs raised independent peace-keeping regiments to watch over the Highlands and, together, these separate regiments became known as The Highland Watch. Over the years they became known simply as The Watch. In 1678, their name changed again to reflect the very dark tartan the soldiers wore. Their plaids were of black, very dark blue and deep forest green tartan, of which the name was the black watch.

By the eighteenth century, there were ten regiments serving under the all-encompassing title of the Black Watch and, in 1740, it was decided to merge them all into one formidable regiment. The official amalgamation took place at Aberfeldy, the area in which Burns composed his superb poem, 'The Birks of Aberfeldy'.

This impressive monument was erected almost 150 years after the formation of the regiment, in commemoration of their great work and history of military excellence. It was unveiled in 1887 by the Marquis of Breadalbane. From his superior vantage point, the lone Highlander looks down upon the winding shape of the River Tay, guarding all those who come beneath his gaze with the protection of the Black Watch.

Commando Memorial
NEAR SPEAN BRIDGE INVERNESS-SHIRE

The Commando Memorial, seen here evocatively through an enveloping mist, is a sobering reminder of a recent, bloodthirsty episode in history. The monument is superbly sculpted from bronze by the artist Scott Sutherland and was unveiled in 1952. It holds three statues, soldiers from the Second World War, frozen in time to commemorate those whose lives ended far too early. The soldiers are looking to the west – to the land on which once stood the training ground of the Commandos.

The training location was chosen for its wilderness and thankless terrain, it is an area that has long seen humans battling against its elements and taking cover in the impenetrability of the trees – it was one of the places that Bonnie Prince Charlie hid himself after Culloden.

Not far from the war memorial stands Spean Bridge, built in 1819 by Thomas Telford, who built more than 1200 bridges throughout Scotland. He also created an incredible causeway of canals, connecting almost every loch in the land. From the bridge one can see the full majesty of Ben Nevis and the Nevis ranges.

Robert the Bruce's Stone
GLEN TROOL GALLOWAY

This stone, dedicated to the great Scottish leader, Robert the Bruce, was erected to commemorate an English defeat of the fourteenth century. The stone overlooks the spectacular scenery of the depths and banks of Galloway's Loch Trool. The loch is surrounded by densely wooded hills and mountains, the perfect area for Robert the Bruce and his men to hide from the unwitting English.

In 1306, the English army, still hoping to defeat the Scots and annex their country, were beaten by Bruce who had the exceptional advantage of altitude. From the summit of a hill overlooking Loch Trool, the very spot at which this memorial now stands, Bruce gave his supporters the order to dislodge boulders lying nearby. With a relentless show of strength he and his men gathered many of the large stones available and hurled them down the hillside at the soldiers attempting to climb up. This monument, constructed from many stones taken from the shore of Loch Trool, is a fitting memorial to the story.

Robert the Bruce Plaque
BANNOCKBURN STIRLING REGION

Robert the Bruce was reputedly born at Turnberry Castle in 1274, although there are no records to confirm this – as a consequence there has been much dispute about the true place of his birth. Robert was born into a wealthy, aristocratic family who hailed from Norman stock and owned a great deal of land in both Scotland and England. Although he spent much of his childhood and early adulthood at court in England, when King Edward I tried to gain control of a Scotland left monarchless by the death of Margaret, the Maid of Norway, Bruce fought for his country's rights against the marauding English.

This plaque and statue to Robert the Bruce are at Bannockburn, near Stirling, the site of a great battle in which he led his army to victory over the English in 1314. Despite the superior numbers of the English forces, Bruce led his men, mostly armed simply with pikes, and shattered the English defence. The besieged Stirling Castle was regained for Scotland.

Eildon Hills
NEAR BREMERSYDE THE BORDERS

The Eildon Hills, in the distance in this photograph, are seen here from the vantage point of William Wallace's statue, looking towards his commemorative urn. It is said that beneath the three resplendent hills lie secrets from millennia past.

The hills are associated with magic and mystery in many forms and are the fabled site of remarkable happenings in several local legends. Some say that the hills were once used as seats in the time when giants used to roam the earth, others say that the hills are the haunt of fairies able to endow humans with great gifts. One such blessed mortal was a thirteenth-century poet, Thomas Learmont. He is fabled to have been the lover of the fairy queen who, in return, granted him the ability to see into the future. His many rhymes were reputed to have been prophetic.

One of the most popular legends to concern the hills is of that elusive founder of Camelot – King Arthur. Many myths surround the monarch whose fame is international, but of whom no concrete evidence has ever been found. One explanation for this lack of physical evidence is that King Arthur, the knights of the round table, and the members of his court, lie slumbering here, beneath Eildon Hills.

Culloden Battlefield Memorial
INVERNESS-SHIRE

The Battle of Culloden was the death knell of the Jacobite cause. In April 1746, the Scottish supporters of Bonnie Prince Charlie, also known as the Young Pretender, were viciously suppressed by the better-equipped, less weary and much larger English army. The battle lasted just forty minutes, and was the last battle to be fought on British soil. In spite of its short duration, 1200 Highlanders were slain by the Duke of Cumberland's soldiers on Culloden's desolate moor.

The prince escaped the battlefield as did many of his surviving supporters – though just a fraction of the men who had so gallantly followed him, and the

hopes of their country, into battle. Although many of his troops were determined to keep up the war, still certain they could win, Charlie was, by now, a spiritless man. He had little fight or hope left and even less money to pay his men. On 20 September 1746, the Young Pretender set sail again for France, never to return.

The memorial seen in this picture bears the following words:

The Battle of Culloden was fought on this moor 16th April 1746. The graves of the gallant Highlanders who fought for Scotland and Prince Charlie are marked by the names of their clans.

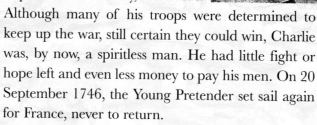

Robert the Bruce Statue
STIRLING STIRLING REGION

This dramatic statue of Robert the Bruce, lit splendidly by the early evening light, is a noble portrait of Scotland's favourite king, who was crowned King of Scotland at Scone in 1306. Despite his exalted position, Bruce spent much of his life in desperate circumstances. The English, furious at the loss of a Scotland so briefly under their control, showed no mercy to the successor of William Wallace. Wallace had been executed as a traitor by King Edward I of England in 1305 and Bruce was hunted relentlessly.

After a horrendous defeat at Methven Park near Perth, in 1306, in which those of Bruce's army to be captured were routinely slaughtered, Bruce became defeated. His wife and daughter had been captured by the English and were imprisoned – for the first four years of her captivity, his daughter was kept in a cage. Bruce himself spent the following year as an outlaw. He was a broken man and entertained thoughts of giving up completely. It is then that he reputedly gained fresh inspiration from a spider inhabiting the same cave as he. The perserverance exhibited by the spider in its tireless web-building, encouraged Bruce to carry on.

Robert the Bruce died in 1329 and is buried at Dunfermline – although his heart lies in Melrose Abbey, at his own request.

Well of Seven Heads
LOCH OICH HIGHLAND REGION

The story of the Well of Seven Heads is one of murder and revenge. The chief of the Keppoch clan sent his two young sons to France to be educated. On their return in 1663, the two boys were murdered at Roybridge. The murderers were their uncles – seven of them to kill just two small boys – greedy to take possession of the power that had passed to the boys on their father's death.

One of the members of the Clan Keppoch was also one of the greatest Gaelic poets of all time, Iain Lom. As well as being the Keppoch bard, Lom was also a fervent activist and, out-raged at the barbarous act, he swore to exact vengeance for his dead chief. After enlisting help from within the clan, he tracked down the seven assassins and chopped off their heads. He and his men took the heads back to show the new chief at Glengarry, washing them on the way in Loch Oich. The place has now become known as the Well of Seven Heads and the monument stands as a fierce reminder of the murders and their revenge.

War Memorial
LEWIS OUTER HEBRIDES

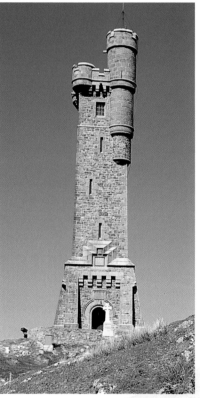

This striking tower overlooks the town of Stornoway – the largest town on the island of Lewis. It is a war memorial, of particular poignancy. The communities of Lewis and Harris suffered drastically through both World Wars: in proportion to their populations, Lewis and Harris lost more men that any other area in the British Isles.

This tower, at the top of Ladyhill, was designed by the architect J. H. Gall of Inverness, and opened by Lord Leverhulme in 1920; this act was Lord Leverhulme's last public duty. The islands of both Lewis and Harris were bought by Lord Leverhulme in 1918. He had grand schemes to bring the islands up-to-date and create great wealth for the people – sadly few of his plans ever took off and he died just seven years after buying the islands.

The monument at Ladyhill was dedicated to the memory of all those who died in the First World War and bears the lengthy inscription of over 1000 names; three decades later, the names of all those killed in the Second World War were added too. All whose names are included on the monument had set out to war from the shores of Lewis.

Jacobite Monument
GLENFINNAN LOCH SHIEL HIGHLAND REGION

This arresting monument marks the spot where Bonnie Prince Charlie's Jacobite campaign began; the campaign which was to end so horrifically at the Battle of Culloden. Prince Charlie was campaigning to reclaim the British throne for the House of Stuart.

On 19 August 1745, a brave young Highlander raised the standard of Prince Charles Edward Stuart, the Young Pretender, and thus began the Jacobite rebellion known now, simply as 'the Forty-Five'. It is possible to climb up the monument by a staircase within its pedestal. On reaching the top, one comes face to face with a statue of the valiant soldier. The monument was not erected until 1815, by a Macdonald, one of the descendants of the clan chief whose support had been the first Bonnie Prince Charlie had received after his journey from France.

Each year, a highland gathering and games are held at this spot to mark the anniversary of one of Scotland's most memorable events.

English Stone
CULLODEN INVERNESS-SHIRE

In 1746, the English forces were led into battle at Culloden by William, Duke of Cumberland – since that day he has been known as 'Butcher Cumberland' by the ancestors of the 1200 Highlanders slain by his forces. The battle has come to be remembered as the worst example of English suppression of the Scots throughout history.

Despite their country's resounding victory over Bonnie Prince Charlie's Jacobite army, there were many English soldiers who were also slain in Culloden's frenzied fighting. This humble stone recalls the less fortunate of an otherwise jubilant army. The inscription simply reads:

Field of the English.
They were buried here.

After their success, the overjoyed English named a flower after their victorious army's leader, they called it 'Sweet William'; the Scots re-named the same flower 'Stinking Willie'. To this day, an annual memorial service is held on the moor every April, on the Saturday closest to the anniversary.

Statue of William Wallace
NEAR ST BOSWELLS THE BORDERS

After rising up in protest against the English regime headed by King Edward I, William Wallace began the life of an outlaw. In 1297 he had murdered an Englishman, William Heselrig, a sheriff of Edward's government. Many accounts of this murder claim that the death of Heselrig was a vengeance killing – an eye for an eye after Heselrig had killed Wallace's lover. Whatever the motive, Wallace was now a wanted man and Edward I was a cruel, bloodthirsty ruler, to whom the Scots nobility were just thorns in the side of his intended new kingdom.

After the Battle of Stirling Bridge, in which Wallace's men defeated the English, Wallace was declared Guardian of Scotland. He was a superb warrior, and may have been a trained soldier – although this is purely speculation as concrete evidence about Wallace's life is scant. Either way, he was an experienced and inspirational leader. After several rousing victories over the English, Wallace was defeated by Edward's army at Falkirk in 1298.

After Falkirk, Wallace escaped capture, heading for the hills where he stayed hidden for seven years. In 1305, he was betrayed to the English and executed as a traitor.

RELICS FROM THE PAST

The history of the islands and mainland of Scotland reaches back over several millennia; in passing these eras have left a rich legacy of relics from the past, both man-made and naturally formed.

Sandstone Sea Arch
NEAR TORNESS EAST LOTHIAN

The incredible, almost surreal, beauty of this sandstone arch is accentuated by the perfection of Scotch evening light. The natural sculpture is one of many such arches on this distinctive stretch of East Lothian coastline, and can only be reached by foot. The absence of vehicles and other modern trappings helps the area retain a timeless atmosphere and fills onlookers with a sense of awe for a structure that has been created over thousands of years. The arch is honed from the rich, red sandstone cliffs, shaped by the power of the sea and the motion of the wind.

The history of Lothian spans settlements from the Stone, Bronze and Iron Ages. At the time of the Pictish culture, the Lothian area is known to have been a separate kingdom and, in the same way as the Borders (in later centuries) became sparring grounds for the English and Scottish, Lothian was fiercely passed between Pict and Northumbrian rulers. In more recent history, the area is best known for its most famous inhabitant, Mary, Queen of Scots.

Cairn Holy Number One
KIRKDALE GLEN GALLOWAY

This distinctive burial chamber in Kirkdale Glen, overlooking Wigtown bay, dates from the Neolithic period. It has come to be known as 'Cairn Holy Number One'. Chambered cairns, such as this one, were common burial places between *c.* 4000 BC and *c.* 2750 BC. The tombs were made up of deeply sunken stone chambers, marked above the earth's surface by cairns. Corpses were taken to the underground chamber through access catacombs. Cairns dating from this era denote mass graves, containing generation after generation of community members.

Galloway has a rich history; its name originates from the Gaelic for 'stranger Gaels' reflecting the early inhabitants' arrival from foreign shores or kingdoms. The region around Kirkdale Glen seems to have been a site of continued human interest since the first strangers settled their families here. Not far from Cairn Holy Number One are two ruined castles, both dating from the sixteenth century. Nearby stands an ancient abbey, a captivating edifice which has dominated its site for almost a thousand years and, just a few miles away, resides a church in which are housed the bones of St Cuthbert.

Stone Circle
CALLANISH LEWIS OUTER HEBRIDES

Callanish's awe-inspiring cluster of stones is just one of several stone circles in Scotland, but this formation is the largest and most impressive of them all. At the centre of the circle stands a lone megalith, extending to sixteen feet in height, and surrounded by thirteen standing stones. From this inner circle radiate four lines of stones, indicating, it has been discovered, the four major directions of the compass. The three lines that extend to the east, south and west are composed of just five stones, but the north-pointing line is a magnificent avenue made up of nineteen stones.

The stones were placed here some time between 2900 BC and 2600 BC. This means that the site at Callanish began later than the earliest preparations at England's Stonehenge, but was finished before the latter's final circle was completed. According to archaeologists, Callanish was excavated and recreated during the Bronze Age and, between 1200 BC and 800 BC, religious rituals appear to have been carried out here. There is too little evidence to be able to determine exactly what these circles were for, presumably ancient pagan rituals, such as the Druidic rites believed to have been carried out at Stonehenge.

Standing Stone
LOCH CRAIGNISH ARGYLLSHIRE

This impressive monolith at the side of Loch Craignish stands beside the remains of burial cairns, which date back for several millennia. Cairns are a common site in Scotland and other countries with races of Celtic origin. They are created simply, from local stones heaped into a mound. Cairns are used to mark a specific site, either a place of historic interest or, as with this one, the hidden depths of underground burial chambers.

This standing stone, atmospherically lit by a cloud-filtered sunset, is a dramatic testament to an era gone by and a sharp reminder of how every generation believes itself to be the pinnacle of human development. Precisely how stones of such massive proportions came to be placed in upright positions have baffled archaeologists and scientists for centuries. It is generally accepted that the construction must have involved machinery of some description, but solid evidence has never been discovered. Even more awe-inspiring is the fact that these human-created monoliths have endured through floods, fire, human devastation and two World Wars.

Templewood Stone Circle
NEAR SLOCKAVULLIN ARGYLLSHIRE

There are two stone circles at this site in Argyll, one of which dates back to the Stone Age and the other to the Bronze Age. The northernmost circle of the two was the first to be discovered by archaeologists, during an excavation which took place in the 1970s. The north circle is also the earlier of the two, it was constructed sometime around 3000 BC.

The area surrounding the Templewood site has a wonderfully rich history spanning many epochs in human development. Nearby are the three Nether Largie cairns (south, mid, and north) and Glebe Cairn. The closest of these to the circles is the Nether Largie south cairn, which has been discovered to have been a central part of funerary proceedings during both the Stone and Bronze Ages. According to archaeologists and historians, Stone Age peoples cremated their dead, whereas those from the Bronze Age buried their corpses; examples of both types of these practices have been discovered at this cairn.

Celtic Cross
IONA INNER HEBRIDES

Angel nor saint have I seen, but I have heard the roar of the western sea, and the isle of my heart is in the midst of it.

St Columba

It was here, the peaceful island of Iona, that St Columba came, settled and established a Christian centre. His doctrines attracted widespread interest, affecting the way in which Celtic peoples had been living their lives. A clever diplomat, as well as a staunch pillar of faith, Columba infiltrated the Pictish culture and helped to unite much of the land. His community flourished for 200 years, until the Columbans finally gave way to the pressure of the new Roman church and retreated from Iona. As a result, the centre of Christianity in Scotland moved to St Andrews.

This perfect example of a Celtic cross dates from the time of Columban supremacy. High crosses are a common feature of early Celtic Christianity, especially in Scotland and Ireland. The ring that encircles the four arms of the cross has been given several explanations. One is that the circles represents Christ's halo; another is that the circle, together with the straight lines of the cross, forms a chi-rho symbol; the third, less spiritual, explanation is that it is simply a structural addition, to prevent the cross from crumbling.

KIRK O' FOREST
SELKIRK THE BORDERS

This small church on the Scottish Borders marks an important site in the country's history: the site at which William Wallace was proclaimed Guardian of Scotland in 1297, after defeating the English at the Battle of Stirling Bridge.

This was not the first time Scotland had been ruled by 'guardians'. In 1286 King Alexander III died leaving his three-year-old granddaughter as his only heir. There were many discussions between the country's most influential figures, resulting in the decision to appoint six guardians to rule until the infant Margaret had reached the age of majority.

The six chosen men provided a harmonious balance, spanning the most powerful families in the land. All continued smoothly until Margaret died, just four years after her grandfather. Civil war ensued with loyalties divided between the two contenders to the throne: John Balliol and Robert the Bruce; Wallace supported Balliol. This chaos was exacerbated by King Edward I of England who was determined to annex Scotland to his kingdom – there followed a period of unrest and oppression, earning Edward the nickname of 'the hammer of the Scots'. William Wallace fell foul of the English regime, and spent the rest of his life as an outlaw. It was during this time that he was declared Scotland's guardian at Kirk O'Forest.

Village Cross

SCONE PALACE PERTHSHIRE

This intricately carved cross was once the centre-piece of the village of Scone. The cross, which dates back to the fifteenth century, can now be seen in the gardens of Scone Palace, close to the graveyard. The thirteen-foot-high cross is an enduring testimony of the skills of Scotland's medieval stonemasons and an outstanding work of Christian art. Although the stem shows several battlescars from five centuries of standing in the village centre, the carvings at the head of the cross are almost unscathed.

Scone Palace dates back to the first years of the nineteenth century when the building was created around the remains of an earlier palace. Today the palace is one of Scotland's premier tourist attractions housing an amazing array of artistic treasures.

The village of Scone has played an important part in Scots history since the time of the Celts. Originally a Christian community with strong links to the country's government, Scone became Scotland's political centre in the ninth century. The village is traditionally associated with the coronation of kings, a tradition begun by St Columba, who crowned the Pictish king, Aidan, in 574, using the stone known as 'Columba's Pillow', later to be known as the 'Stone of Scone'.

Westport

ST ANDREWS FIFE PENINSULA

Westport was the main entrance to the old city of St Andrews: the forbidding gateway is dated 1589, although its side arches and coat of arms were added in 1840. This well-preserved example of medieval architecture is one of a very small number of city gates still standing in Scotland.

St Andrew is the patron saint of Scotland and the story of his martyrdom gave the Scots their flag – a diagonal white cross against a blue background. In *c.* AD 69, a Christian named Andrew was crucified for his beliefs. He asked to be executed on a diagonal cross, because he felt unworthy to die in the same manner as Jesus Christ. The body of the martyr, later to be beatified, was buried in Patras, Greece until his remains were brought to Scotland – landing at the place now named St Andrews – in the eighth century.

Today the town is best-known for its university and golf course. Built in 1412, the illustrious university is the oldest in Scotland with a history of academic excellence. The more leisurely site of the golf course is a luxurious three-quarters of a mile long and renowned throughout the international golfing world.

Stenton Village
EAST LOTHIAN

The old village of Stenton dates back to the sixteenth century and is protected by law. The village has two greens, each of which has its own well. The green at the east side of Stenton houses a 'tron', a form of weighing scales, used for weighing wool after the shearing of the sheep had taken place, as such it was a vital part of the village's life. Most buildings in Stenton date from the sixteenth through to the nineteenth century, the oldest is the old parish church, built in 1525. All that is left of the church now is a vault and tower.

Other buildings include the new church, built in 1828 to a Gothic plan; the old manse (priest's residence) which was built in 1783, struck by lightning in 1820 and repaired shortly afterwards; a bakehouse; a schoolhouse; a joiner's house and several houses.

The dovecot (as seen to the rear of the photograph) was an important part of rural life. Before the eighteenth-century introduction of root vegetables, the only animals villagers could afford to keep alive through the harsh winter months were breeding stock. Superfluous animals were slaughtered and their meat salted. Pigeons remained the only form of fresh meat available in winter.

Village Street
DUNBLANE STIRLING REGION

These sixteenth-century houses in Dunblane capture the very essence of the quiet little town. One of Scotland's most attractive places to live, Dunblane is set among rolling hills and gentle watercourses and the current community retains a strong attachment to their town's history. One of Dunblane's most beautiful attractions is a fifteenth-century bridge. This sturdy structure that crosses the Allan Water, has been a central part of life here since 1409.

The focal point of the town is its ancient cathedral, which was built over the twelfth and thirteenth centuries. The ubiquitous David I (1124–53) proclaimed this area a religious site and built the cathedral in 1150. However, archaeologists have discovered that, long before the reign of David, a church had already been built on this site, one that can be traced as far back in time as the sixth century.

The cathedral which stands in Dunblane today holds a fascinating mystery: moulded into the west wall is a chamber known only as 'Katie Ogie's Hole' – but nothing is known of the elusive Katie Ogie, or why this should have been her hiding place.

Old Mills

ELGIN MORAYSHIRE

The building pictured here is one of Morayshire's most famous historical landmarks. There has been a dwelling, possibly a mill, on this site since the thirteenth century, although this mill was built in the 1600s. Old Mills was originally used for the processing of grain; today the building has been carefully, and faithfully, restored to reflect the life of its former workers and community.

At one time, the region of Moray was an independent kingdom, ruled by a Pictish monarch and politically separate from the rest of the land. The climate in this area is uncharacteristically temperate for its northerly location, making it the ideal place for early settlers, whose survival depended largely on the food they could raise from the land. It was this mild clime which earned Morayshire the name of 'the garden of Scotland'.

The waters of the Moray Firth are also exceptional. When looking out over the sea one can often observe a school of resident bottlenose dolphins, this group is one of only two such schools known to reside in British waters.

Thatched Croft
SOUTH UIST OUTER HEBRIDES

This typical example of a thatched croft, seen here with a stack of peat blocks alongside it, is an evocative glimpse of history. A croft is a house on a small farm or tract of land, rented from a landlord and worked by the tenant. A crofter's existence was a hard, often fairly thankless one, and subsistence was achieved by spectacularly hard labour and thorough knowledge of the land. Crofts and the land rented to the tenant for his own use, were usually in places where good soil was scarce and harsh landscapes were common – any decent land would be used as farmland by the landlord.

When seen from the air, the land around old crofting communities is a sculptured pattern that holds the history of its residents in its indentations. Crofters in island areas such as North Uist, would have 'lazy beds', their own slither of land in which they would grow potatoes, turnips and whatever other vegetables were possible. In coastal areas, they would cut strips of land between the rocks, fertilising the soil with nutrient-rich seaweed and growing as varied a diet as they could.

Peat is always stacked in the way shown in this photograph, this is to ensure that any potentially ruinous rain can drain away.

Prince's Cairn
LOCH NAM UAMH LOCHABER INVERNESS-SHIRE

The term 'Loch nam Uamh' translates to mean the 'Loch of the Caves', indicative of of the many rock fissures at its banks. Crevices such as these played an invaluable part in the life of itinerant Highlanders, providing welcome respite from the rigours of an exposed Scots night.

The site commemorated here is the spot at which, on 25 July 1745, Bonnie Prince Charlie arrived from France, with just seven men. He had intended to return to Scotland with an entire army, but to the disappointment of his supporters, appeared with fewer than a shinty team. He had

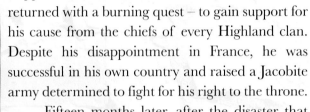

returned with a burning quest – to gain support for his cause from the chiefs of every Highland clan. Despite his disappointment in France, he was successful in his own country and raised a Jacobite army determined to fight for his right to the throne.

Fifteen months later, after the disaster that was the Battle of Culloden, Bonnie Prince Charlie returned to this very site. This poignant cairn marks the spot from which he left Scotland's soil forever, leaving his supporters to the murderous hands of his, and their, enemies.

First House and Marriage Rooms
GRETNA GREEN DUMFRIESSHIRE

The First House in Scotland, also called the Old Toll Bar, dates back to the nineteenth century; the Marriage Rooms, within the house, precede their facade by about one hundred years.

The very words 'Gretna Green' have become synonymous with elopement. Before 1940, the marriage laws in Scotland differed vastly from those in England in two important ways. At the time, as is still the case, parental consent was needed in England to marry before the age of eighteen, in Scotland parental consent was not required. More importantly, there was no need of a registrar or member of the clergy to perform a ceremony; all the devoted couple had to do was declare themselves husband and wife before two witnesses. From that moment on, the marriage was legal. The reason for Gretna Green's popularity was its location – it was the first attainable place in Scotland for couples fleeing opposing parents in England.

To this day, the marriage rooms at Gretna Green remain a popular place for weddings, though elopement is less common.

Birthplace of Flora MacDonald
SOUTH UIST OUTER HEBRIDES

Flora MacDonald lived between 1722 and 1790. She was born on the small island of South Uist, where this cairn now marks the place of her birth. A staunch Jacobite and heroine of Scottish folklore, she was one of the most influential helpers in the escape of Bonnie Prince Charlie after the disastrous battle of Culloden in 1746. She dressed the Prince as a woman, claimed him as her serving maid and travelled with him to Skye where they said their last goodbye.

Flora MacDonald suffered for her loyalty to the Young Pretender. She was arrested by the Hanoverian government and imprisoned: first in Dunstaffnage Castle, before she was transported to a prison ship near Edinburgh and then on to London.

In 1774, after her release from captivity, Flora emigrated to America with her husband, Allan MacDonald. She lived in North Carolina, but remained for only five years before the draw of her native land became too strong. In 1779 she returned to Scotland where she remained until her death at the age of 68.

Thatched Croft
NORTH UIST OUTER HEBRIDES

Crofters' lives changed dramatically in the eighteenth and nineteenth centuries, when landlords (most of whom were resident in England or in Scotland's cities) decided their land would be more lucrative if used to raise cattle and sheep, rather than housing tenants. This meant forcible eviction, often causing entire communities to emigrate to the 'New World'. The residents of one such village were re-housed in atrocious conditions by the wife of the laird; her reason for demolishing their homes was that they spoilt her view!

In 1882, a change took place. At the small Skye village of Braes, an indignant group of crofters refused to obey their landlord's orders to leave their homes. They defied him and the policemen who arrived to serve eviction notices, and demanded rights. Fights ensued between police and crofters and the national press took up the story – the result of ensuing outside interest was the passing of the Crofters' Act of 1886. This act of parliament disallowed landlords the right of eviction on a whim and granted enforceable rights to crofters.

Loch Erishort
ISLE OF LEWIS OUTER HEBRIDES

Of all the crofting communities in Scotland, those on the islands had perhaps the most difficult lives. Being in a distant geographical position meant that they were often completely isolated from the potential support of neighbouring communities. This, combined with the islands' relative smallness meant they were generally forgotten by those in power in Edinburgh. As a result the crofters of Hebridean islands were utterly dependant on the goodwill and humanity of their laird.

This cairn, sited at the west end of Lewis's Loch Erishort, was erected to commemorate the deer park raiders of 1887. The raiders were members of a crofting community whose disinterested, grasping landlord's behaviour was intolerable. Despite the Crofter's Act of 1882, their living conditions were appalling and little improvement had been made in their general circumstances. Frustrated in every attempt to gain fair treatment

from the immovable laird, a group of tenants camped in his park. In an anguished bid to draw attention to their desperate plight, the raiders slew around 200 of the laird's deer.

Scotland Past and Present

J. Blaeu's map of Scotland was drawn up in 1645, during the reign of King Charles II (1630–85). Blaeu was one of the western world's foremost cartographers and his work was executed in fine detail, featuring famous landmarks and distinct geographical regions.

Scotland has changed a great deal since the seventeenth century and the place names echo that disparity. Many of the names shown on this map hark back to a time when the Celtic language was much more widely spoken and Scotland was divided into smaller regions than it is today. Detailed below are the modern regions* with their seventeenth-century names; these are followed by the page numbers on which the photographs can be found.

Aberdeenshire *(Mernis)*
142

Angus *(Angus)*
82, 105, 132

Argyllshire *(Movern, Laern, Knap)*
14, 16, 17, 23, 24, 28, 31, 38, 39,
40, 43, 48, 51, 54, 56, 57, 58, 60,
95, 100, 101, 106, 114, 138, 145,
150, 180, 181

Ayrshire *(Kylle)*
72, 130, 133

The Borders *(Teviotdaill, Merche, Selkirk, Liddisdail, Annendail)*
74, 83, 84, 85, 89, 115, 122, 123,
124, 125, 126, 152, 165, 173, 183

Caithness *(Cat tenes)*
108, 109, 141, 151

Dumfriesshire *(Andail)*
80, 128, 192

Edinburgh *(Edinburgh)*
70, 71, 76, 104, 112, 120, 127

Fife Peninsula *(Fyffe)*
66, 144, 185

Galloway *(Galloway, Nithis)*
88, 94, 163, 178

Glasgow *(Clyds Dail)*
67, 68, 69, 77, 110

Hebrides *(Hebrides)*
20, 21, 22, 25, 26, 29, 50, 86, 92,
139, 160, 170, 179, 182, 189,
193, 194, 195

Highland Region *(Strathnavern)*
37, 49, 59. 61, 63, 169, 171

Inverness-shire *(Glen Garrif, Glen Slifh-Garrow, Murray, Ross)*
30, 36, 41, 42, 44, 90, 107, 116,
136, 143, 147, 149, 153, 155,
162, 166, 172

Lothian *(Lothian, Twaddail)*
103, 117, 146, 148, 154, 176, 186

Morayshire *(Murray)*
188

Nairnshire *(Murray)*
102

Perthshire *(Strath-Ern, Fyffe, Angus)*
18, 19, 34, 62, 75, 98, 131, 161,
184

Renfrewshire *(Renfrew)*
91

Stirling Region *(Sterlin Shyr)*
27, 45, 87, 158, 164, 168, 187

Strathclyde *(Clyds Dail)*
113

Sutherland *(Sowtherland, Assynt Coy-gach)*
46, 47, 111, 140

The regions of Scotland are currently in the process of changing. Those defined in this book are according to local Tourist Information offices.

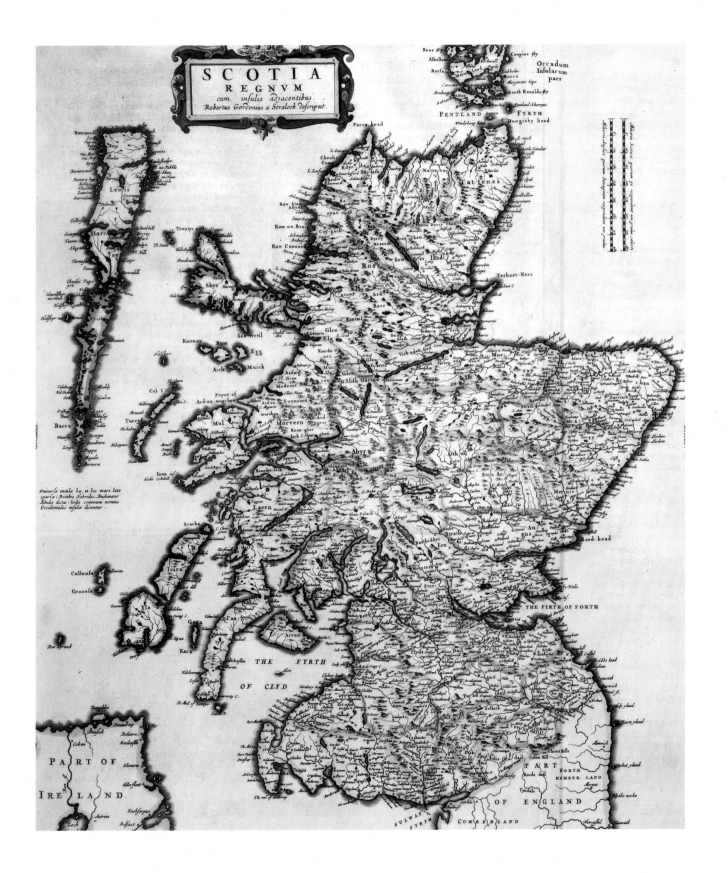

Index